"Tommy Tang is to Asian Cuisine
what Wolfgang Puck is to California style pizza."

Dotty Griffith,
Dallas Morning News

modern thai cuisine

". . .Variety is the TANG of life!"

Susan Jaques,
LA Times

modern thai cuisine

"Tommy Tang is a legend by now,
after years of pioneering in the field of
Thai/Oriental/Western Cuisine"

Rose Dosti
LA Times

". . .innovative, eclectic flavor that
pleases the palate. . ."

LA Times Magazine

Tommy Tang's
Modern
Thai Cuisine

TOMMY TANG'S
MODERN
THAI CUISINE

SQUAREONE 1
PUBLISHERS

Square One Publishers
115 Herricks Road • Garden City Park, NY 11040
(516) 535-2010 • (877) 900-BOOK
www.squareonepublishers.com

A portion of this book's revenue will be donated to the Tsunami Children
Foundation. To learn more about this foundation, see page 129.

Library of Congress Cataloging-in-Publication Data

Tang, Tommy
    Tommy Tang's modern Thai cuisine / Tommy Tang.
        p. cm.
    Originally published: New York : Doubleday, 1991.
    Includes index.
    ISBN 0-7570-0254-4
        1. Cookery, Thai. I. Title: Modern Thai Cuisine. II. Title.

TX724.5.T5T36 2005
641.59593–dc22

                            2005048973

ILLUSTRATIONS BY HUGH HARRISON

INTERIOR PHOTOGRAPHY BY LOIS ELLEN FRANK

BOOK DESIGN BY CAROL MALCOLM-RUSSO

Printed in Hong Kong

10   9   8   7   6   5   4   3   2   1

CONTENTS

THIS BOOK IS DEDICATED TO MY MOTHER, SUDA (1925–1988)

My dearest mother,
Let's go to visit your favorite place,
stay at your favorite hotel,
shop at your favorite stores.
Let's go to dinner at your favorite restaurant,
eat your favorite food, drink your favorite tea.
Let's talk about the old days,
good times and hard times,
when we would cry and laugh.
And let's spend time together
and be happy forever.
These are all the things I'd like to do—
if the words could be true,
the reality would never be so blue.

Love, your son,
Tommy Tang

ACKNOWLEDGMENTS

Special thanks to my wife Sandi, who painfully lifted this project off the ground and endured many hours of aggravation from me. She pushed, encouraged, and kept the book alive through all the uncertain times. Without her hard work and support it would have taken much, much longer to see this volume published; she's the soul behind the book, for which I am very grateful.

Photographer Lois Frank employed great imagination and skill, with eyes as sharp as an eagle's looking through the lens. Her photos truly turned my dishes into works of art.

Food stylist Norman Stewart has a perfect understanding of how dishes should reflect the person who created them. He made the food look so attractive and mouth-watering that it practically jumps off the plate.

Spend a day with cover photographer Anthony Loew and you'll find that he can make you look a lot better.

Makeup artist Tina Austin may have found that it's not easy to make a chef look his best, but thanks to her talents I'm considerably more presentable.

Thanks to my kitchen staffs, in both Los Angeles and New York, for assisting me with testing and perfecting the recipes.

Without the support and inspiration of my friends and patrons who frequent my restaurants, volunteered for recipe testing, and supported this project, there would be no Tommy Tang's and I would never have gotten a cookbook off the ground. I thank you all from the bottom of my heart.

Thanks to designers Carol Malcom-Russo and Eric Ayzenberg for the creativity that has made this book so exceptionally handsome.

China, glassware, and utensils by Annieglass Studio in Santa Cruz, California, and Tesoro in Los Angeles made stunning settings for my food. Sue Dorman, also of Los Angeles, kindly supplied chopsticks.

Thanks to Patricia Connell for her commitment to and belief in this book. She spent many hours making the recipes easy to follow and understand; there were times when we had to go through the manuscript with a critical eye while at the same time looking after her two and my two children. I sincerely thank her for her time and effort in making this the best book it can be.

A WORD FROM TOMMY

Cooking is an easy way to relieve stress—or at least I hear that some people say so. Who, I wonder? All I know is that cooking can be fun and entertaining; it is a way to go back to basics; and cooking at home can do a world of good for the family budget.

When was the last time you invited friends or neighbors to come over for a home-cooked meal? I can already hear the answer: Who has time? Who has the energy? It's easier to dine out or to get something delivered. Sure, restaurants and takeout are convenient—but who ever said that convenience is better for you? Even if you can afford to dine out every night, that's not the point.

You won't have to rush out to buy special utensils to prepare my modern Thai cuisine. Use whatever pots and pans you already have in the kitchen; I don't even use a wok myself. Consider this book a set of simple guidelines, and don't be afraid to substitute other ingredients wherever you wish. Trial and error will make you an expert on Thai cooking and will allow you to create your own new dishes.

As you'll readily see in thumbing through the recipes, I use a number of ingredients that are not indigenous to Thailand's cooking, preferring to mix the best of East and West into my own lighter, simpler, and more versatile cuisine. Such ingredients as rosemary, arugula, cream, pine nuts, and olive oil do not belong to the standard Thai repertoire, but I find that they enhance it immensely. Additions like these put my own personal stamp on the recipes, not to mention making them uniquely delicious. And ingredients that may be unfamiliar are defined in the Glossary, which precedes the recipes.

You will also notice that I have not included any desserts in this book. Plenty of cookbooks have great dessert recipes, and I wanted to give all the space I had to presenting my own Thai cuisine. Nothing makes a better dessert for a Thai meal than a tempting bowl of fresh fruit (the more exotic, the better), but if you know of a terrific patisserie, who's to say no?

Now that you've bought this cookbook, don't let it sit on the shelf. I really want to encourage you to use it. The recipes are easy to follow, and it's especially enjoyable to let others participate in preparing the meal. You'll get to know your friends—even your mate—better if you cook together; you will find that you talk about things that wouldn't otherwise come up, and it will make you closer. Invite your parents over for a meal; this is a pleasure that money can't buy.

One thing I deeply regret is that I will never again be able to prepare a meal for my own mom. I urge you not to have the same regrets. Enjoy cooking for your family; forget about convenience; spend more time in the kitchen and create some great meals. Bon appétit.

Please note: All recipes in this book serve 4 people, unless otherwise indicated. You can double the recipe to serve 8, or halve it to serve 2.

modern thai cuisine

GLOSSARY OF INGREDIENTS

bamboo shoots: available canned in various forms—whole, in chunks, sliced, shredded, and in strips. I find the strips easiest to use, and they are what the recipes in this book call for.

basil, Thai: darker in color, stronger in aroma, and spicier in flavor than regular basil, but otherwise interchangeable with it. A sprig of the flowers makes a nice garnish.

bean condiment, Thai or Chinese: the two types are similar; use either. Made from fermented soybeans, this salty-flavored condiment combines with other ingredients to create a complex, subtle flavor.

bean sauce, Thai sweet black: dark soy sauce with molasses added. It gives a sweet, smoky flavor when added to recipes.

chili paste, fresh: gives a spicy, hot flavor. Also known by its Indonesian name, *sambal oelek*.

chili paste, roasted: important for soups in particular, as well as for many sauces and salad dressings. Made from a combination of ingredients (typically roasted red chilies, garlic, onion, dried shrimp, sugar, fish sauce, and vegetable oil), the paste gives a distinctively tangy, mildly smoky flavor.

curry paste, green: this combination of fresh green chilies, lemon grass, cilantro root, and galanga (see page 2) has a spicy, refreshing flavor.

curry paste, red: similar to green curry paste, but with red chilies.

daikon sprouts: these long, slim sprouts have the spicy flavor of radish. Use in sushi rolls, in salads, and for garnish.

enoki mushrooms: these pure white mushrooms have long, skinny stems and tiny caps. They're beautiful to look at in sushi stuffings, salads, sautés, and soups, and they add a delicate buttery flavor.

1

firm brown tofu: with a flavor resembling baked beans, this is used in pad thai noodles (page 56). Tofu comes in many varieties, but the firm brown kind is always in 3-inch × ½-inch thick squares.

fish sauce, Thai: the basic, most essential Thai seasoning, this is a salty, very aromatic liquid that provides a distinctive flavor.

flying-fish roe: the very small, pinkish-red eggs of the flying fish, commonly used in sushi. Any other similar roe can be substituted—shrimp, lobster, smelt, etc.

galanga: also known as galingale, kha, and laos, this is a root resembling ginger, but with a distinctive flavor, a more translucent skin, and a tinge of pink when fresh.

green mango: unripe mango, which can be used just like green apple; substitute the apple if necessary.

green papaya: tart and crunchy underripe papaya, used mainly in Thai Papaya Salad (page 40).

kaffir lime leaves: glossy, dark green leaves of the kaffir lime tree; they impart a refreshing, mysterious lemon-lime flavor.

kra-chai: a long, slender root, related to ginger, with a flavor that suggests a combination of ginger, turmeric, and galanga. It is sometimes available fresh in Asian markets.

lemon grass: indispensable in Thai cooking, this consists of long, very firm stalks with green tops. The grass has a pronounced lemon flavor and aroma. The stalks will last up to three weeks in the refrigerator, and an average-size stalk yields about 3 tablespoons chopped. Dried lemon grass is also available.

Maggi sauce: the brand name for a Swiss condiment with a distinctive taste that somewhat recalls a mix of soy sauce and mild vinegar. It is not readily available in all areas, so if you have any problems finding it, just leave it out.

Manila clams: these are the sweetest, tenderest clams I've ever tasted, and tend to be not at all gritty.

meekrob noodles: very thin dried rice noodles, known in Thai as *sen-mee*, comparable in thickness to angel hair pasta.

mussamun curry paste: an aromatic combination of cardamom, lemon grass, cinnamon, cloves, and chiles.

nori: dark green sheets of dried Japanese seaweed, used for wrapping sushi.

oyster sauce: this combination of oyster extract, soy sauce, and starch has a mildly salty, fishy flavor. It is a Chinese condiment commonly available in supermarkets.

pad thai noodles: dried rice noodles, known in Thai as *sen chan*. They are available in narrow, medium and wide versions. I prefer the medium ones, which are about the width of linguine.

palm sugar: a coarse brown sugar that is crystallized from the sap of the coconut palm. It is collected much like the sap of maple trees, but the workers have to shinny all the way up to the tops of the palms to do it. The sugar lends a sweet, fruity flavor. If unavailable, substitute honey.

Panang curry paste: the most versatile of all curry pastes, this is a mix of red chilies, onion, garlic, galanga, lemon grass, and kaffir lime. It has a wonderfully interesting, complex flavor.

pickled ginger: a hot, sweet-tart condiment that is served with sushi and to refresh the palate between courses.

plum sauce: a fruity, translucent, sweet-sour sauce that is common in Chinese cooking. Used as a dip for egg rolls, won ton, duck, and many other dishes.

rice noodles, fresh: similar to regular Western noodles, but made wih rice flour. Because rice noodles are already steam-cooked when you buy them, they cook very quickly. Purchase only what you need; even in the refrigerator they last only two or three days.

rice vinegar: clear, a pale straw color, and milder than cider or wine vinegar.

Santa Fe chili powder: rosy red, with a sweet, spicy flavor superior to that of regular chili powder.

sausage, Thai: the same as Chinese sausage, this is a firm pork sausage that resembles a small salami. Made with pork or pork and liver, they are available regular, fatty, or extra-lean.

serrano chilies: small, green, and very hot. Jalapeños or other similar hot chilies can be readily substituted. Be careful never to touch your eyes after handling chilies, because the pungent oils will burn them.

sesame oil, Asian: a brown, aromatic oil made from roasted sesame seeds. Don't substitute the clear, unroasted sesame oil available in natural foods stores; it doesn't have the same rich fragrance or nutty flavor.

shiitake mushrooms: exceptionally meaty and flavorful mushrooms of which only the caps are used. Great either steamed or sautéed.

shrimp powder: made from small shrimp that are dried and coarsely ground; the name "powder" is really a misnomer, but that is how the product is usually labeled. The flavor resembles shrimp in the same way that the flavor of beef jerky resembles beef.

spring-roll skins: paper-thin squares made from wheat flour; similar to but thinner than wonton wrappers. Or use egg-roll skins.

sugarcane juice: expressed from sugarcane, this sweet liquid can be drunk by itself or added to recipes.

tamarind juice: a very sour liquid extracted from tamarind paste or the pod of the tamarind tree. If unavailable, substitute twice the amount of lemon juice.

thin soy sauce: made from yellow soybeans, this is lighter and less salty than regular soy sauce.

Tommy Tang's Thai sate marinade: a combination of olive oil, curry powder, tumeric, cumin, coriander, and garlic that gives mouth-watering flavor to sates, meats, and vegetables.

Tommy Tang's Thai seasoning: a combination of garlic, black pepper, white pepper, chili powder, and cayenne pepper. At the restaurant we use this in almost every marinade and in many sauces. Or try brushing French bread with olive oil, sprinkling on the seasoning, and baking it as you would garlic bread—it's fantastic.

wasabi: dried, powdered, green Japanese horseradish, used to give pungency to sushi. Use sparingly; it's extremely hot.

wonton wrappers: dough squares made from wheat flour and starch; slightly thicker than egg-roll skins.

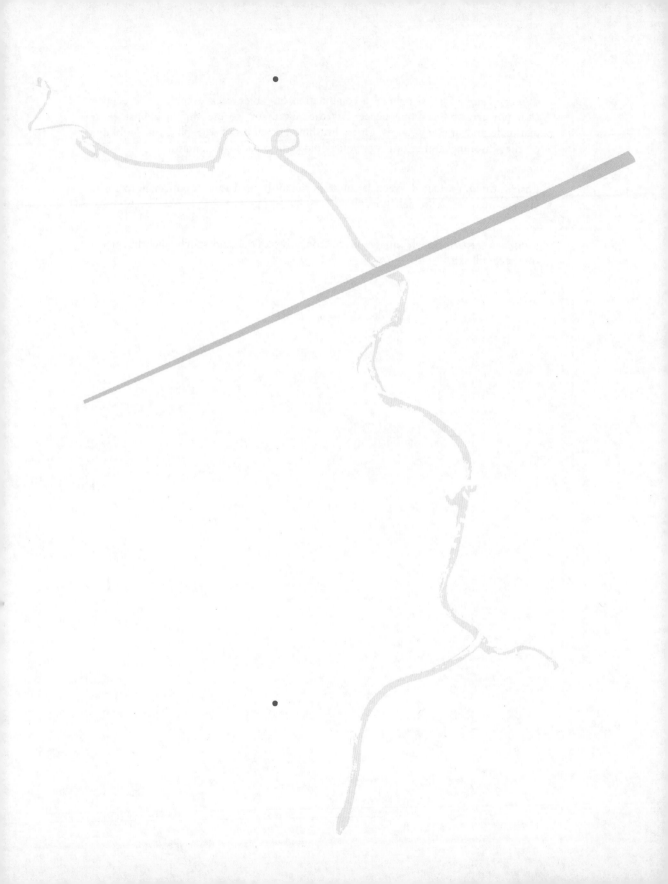

APPETIZERS

Angel Wings

I admit it: to debone the chicken wings you need the patience of an angel (or at least I assume angels have a lot of it). Facing the daily smog problems here in the City of Angels also requires a lot of patience with the EPA . . . and when I feel it wearing thin, I practice building up patience by making more Angel Wings.

8 MEDIUM CHICKEN WINGS

MARINADE

¼ CUP THIN SOY SAUCE

1 TABLESPOON THAI FISH SAUCE

2 TABLESPOONS CHOPPED GARLIC

1 TABLESPOON CHOPPED CILANTRO
ROOT (RESERVE LEAVES)

1 TEASPOON WHITE PEPPER

STUFFING

8 OUNCES GROUND CHICKEN

6 TABLESPOONS CHOPPED BAMBOO
SHOOTS

6 TABLESPOONS CHOPPED SHIITAKE OR
REGULAR MUSHROOMS

¼ CUP CHOPPED ONIONS

¼ CUP DICED SCALLIONS

3 CUPS VEGETABLE OIL (FOR DEEP
FRYING)

CUCUMBER DIP

½ CUP WATER

¼ CUP SUGAR

¼ CUP RICE VINEGAR

1 TABLESPOON PLUM SAUCE

¼ TEASPOON PAPRIKA

⅛ TEASPOON FRESH CHILI PASTE

⅛ TEASPOON SALT

1 CUCUMBER, SEEDED AND CUT INTO
½-INCH DICE

2 TABLESPOONS FINELY DICED
SCALLIONS

2 TABLESPOONS CHOPPED RED ONIONS

1 TABLESPOON CHOPPED CILANTRO
LEAVES (RESERVED FROM MARINADE)

2 TABLESPOONS GROUND UNSALTED
PEANUTS

To bone chicken wings, make a small cut at base of 1 wing; fold down skin to expose bone. Continue folding and pushing skin down until joint is exposed. Using a small, sharp knife, cut cartilage at joint to free large bone; discard bone. Snap cartilage at wing tip to free smaller bone; discard. Smooth skin back into place, forming a tube for stuffing. Repeat with remaining wings.

Combine marinade ingredients in a large bowl and mix well. Add boned chicken wings and stir to coat completely. Cover the bowl and let stand for 1 hour.

Remove wings from marinade and drain, reserving marinade. Add stuffing ingredients to marinade and mix well. Stuff chicken wings with mixture.

Bring water to boil in bottom of steamer. Arrange stuffed wings on steamer rack, cover and steam for 25 minutes. Remove and pat dry. Heat vegetable oil in medium saucepan to 350° F. Add wings in batches and fry until browned on all sides, about 4 to 6 minutes. Remove and drain on paper towels.

To make cucumber dip, combine water, sugar, vinegar, plum sauce, paprika, chili paste, and salt in a small saucepan and bring to boil over high heat. Reduce heat to low and simmer 2 minutes. Remove from heat and let cool. Combine cucumber, scallions, red onions, and cilantro in a serving bowl. Stir in vinegar mixture. Sprinkle with peanuts.

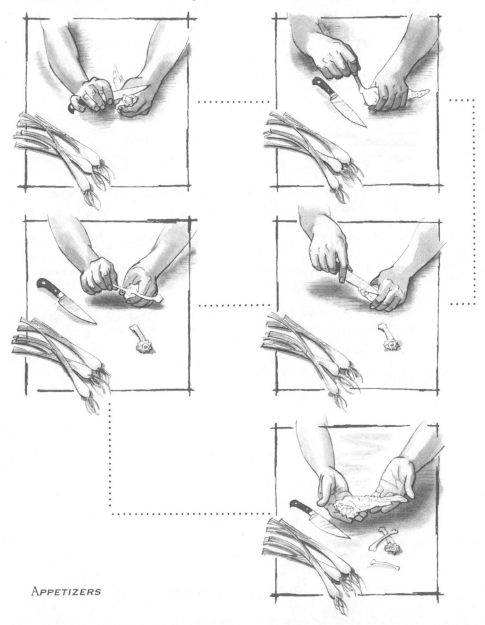

Nam Chicken

From northern Thailand, this appetizer combines simple herbs and spices to sensational effect. Each bite is a mouthful of tangy, peanutty flavor that will have you reaching for more.

1 TEASPOON OLIVE OIL

1 TEASPOON FINELY CHOPPED GARLIC

2 TABLESPOONS LEMON GRASS STOCK OR CHICKEN STOCK (SEE PAGE 110)

6 OUNCES CHICKEN BREAST MEAT, MINCED

¼ CUP WHOLE UNSALTED ROASTED PEANUTS

2 TABLESPOONS THAI FISH SAUCE

2 TABLESPOONS FRESH LIME JUICE

¼ CUP SLICED RED ONIONS

3 TABLESPOONS FINELY DICED SCALLIONS

2 TABLESPOONS FINELY DICED, PEELED FRESH GINGER

2 TABLESPOONS CHOPPED CILANTRO

½ TEASPOON CRUSHED RED PEPPER OR CAYENNE PEPPER

1 SMALL HEAD ROMAINE, GREEN-LEAF, OR ICEBERG LETTUCE, WASHED AND DRIED

Heat oil in a small skillet over medium heat. Add garlic and sauté until golden, about 1½ to 2 minutes. Remove from heat and set aside.

Place a medium skillet over medium heat. Pour in stock and heat for 1 minute. Add chicken and stir for 2 to 3 minutes, or until chicken is cooked and stock is nearly evaporated. Remove from heat; stir in reserved garlic and all remaining ingredients except lettuce.

Separate lettuce leaves; wash and dry. Arrange in a circle on a large platter. To serve, have diners scoop 2 mounds of chicken mixture onto each leaf and fold the leaf over.

THAI TOAST

Back around 1978 and '79, before I opened my own place, I was the chef at another Thai restaurant in Hollywood. An attractive young woman was a regular customer there, and Thai Toast was her favorite dish. It had always been made in squares, but one night she called in advance to say she would be coming in and I had the inspiration to cut the toast into hearts. The rest is history; we were married in 1981. (And by the way, I've made Thai Toast in heart shapes ever since.)

CUCUMBER DIP (SEE PAGE 8)

8 SLICES WHITE BREAD

12 OUNCES MEDIUM SHRIMP (21 TO 25 PER POUND), SHELLED AND DEVEINED

4 OUNCES LEAN GROUND PORK OR CHICKEN

1 EGG

3 TABLESPOONS FINELY DICED SCALLIONS

3 TABLESPOONS CHOPPED CILANTRO

2 TABLESPOONS GRANULATED GARLIC

1½ TABLESPOONS THAI FISH SAUCE

1 TEASPOON WHITE PEPPER

3 CUPS VEGETABLE OIL (FOR DEEP FRYING)

Prepare cucumber dip and set aside at room temperature. Using a heart-shaped cookie cutter, cut out 2 hearts from each slice of bread; set aside.

Finely grind shrimp in a food processor. Transfer to a mixing bowl, add all remaining ingredients except oil, and mix well. Spread evenly over bread hearts.

Heat oil in a deep skillet at 350° F. Place hearts, a few at a time, in oil with topping-side-down and fry 2 minutes. Turn and fry until bread is golden brown. Remove and drain on paper towels, patting tops with another towel to remove excess oil.

Serve toast hot with cucumber dip.

Manhattan Roll

You've probably heard of a California Roll. Since we have a restaurant in New York as well as one in L.A., I wanted to create a sushi that New Yorkers could call their own.

2 CUPS COOKED SUSHI RICE (SEE PAGE 114)

2 SHEETS NORI, CUT IN HALF

1 TABLESPOON WASABI POWDER MIXED WITH 1 TABLESPOON WARM WATER TO MAKE PASTE

1 MEDIUM LOBSTER TAIL, COOKED, SHELLED, AND CUT LENGTHWISE INTO 8 SLICES

1 SMALL PACKET ENOKI MUSHROOMS

1 SMALL PACKET DAIKON SPROUTS

1 2-INCH PIECE CUCUMBER, PEELED, SEEDED, AND CUT INTO JULIENNE

2 TABLESPOONS SESAME SEED

2 TABLESPOONS FLYING-FISH ROE

6 OUNCES PICKLED GINGER (GARNISH)

SOY SAUCE DIP (SEE PAGE 16)

Spread rice smoothly on nori, dividing evenly. Smear rice with wasabi. Using ¼ of the ingredients per roll, top with lobster, mushrooms, daikon sprouts, and cucumber, arranging pieces lengthwise on seaweed. Sprinkle evenly with sesame seed and roe. Working with 1 roll at a time, hold seaweed with both hands and roll up slowly until ends meet. Drape a piece of plastic wrap over roll; top with bamboo sushi mat. Squeeze gently until roll holds together. Remove plastic and bamboo mat.

Dip a very sharp knife into cold water and let excess drip off. Cut each roll into 6 crosswise slices. Arrange on plates and serve with pickled ginger and soy sauce dip.

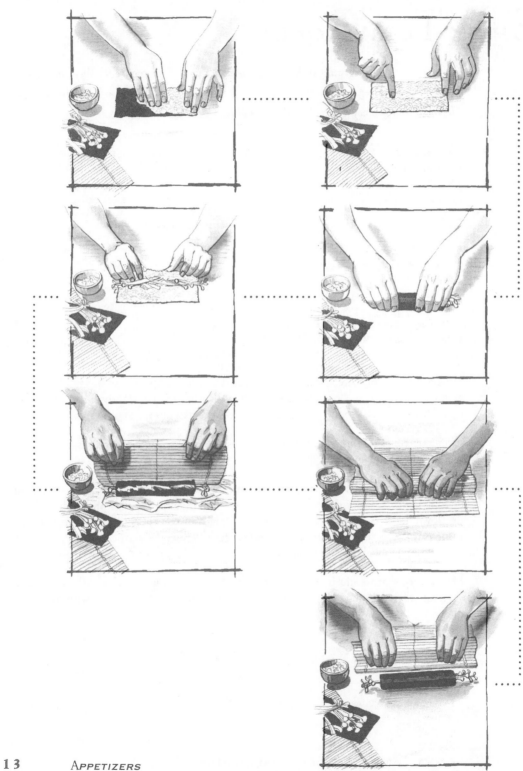

Spicy Tuna Roll

You may be wondering what sushi recipes are doing in a Thai cookbook. Well, as far as I know, Tommy Tang's is the only place in the world where you can find a sushi bar in a Thai restaurant. Spicy Tuna Roll always makes a hit at cocktail parties.

MAYONNAISE
1 MEDIUM EGG WHITE
1 TABLESPOON RICE VINEGAR
¼ TEASPOON WHITE PEPPER
2 TABLESPOONS OLIVE OIL

8 OUNCES FRESH TUNA, GROUND
2 TABLESPOONS FINELY DICED
    SCALLIONS
1 TABLESPOON TOMMY TANG'S THAI
    SEASONING
1 TABLESPOON ASIAN SESAME OIL
1 TABLESPOON SESAME SEED

2 CUPS COOKED SUSHI RICE (SEE
    PAGE 114)
2 SHEETS NORI, CUT IN HALF
1 TABLESPOON WASABI POWDER MIXED
    WITH 1 TABLESPOON WARM WATER TO
    MAKE PASTE

6 OUNCES PICKLED GINGER (GARNISH)
SOY SAUCE DIP (SEE PAGE 16)

To prepare mayonnaise, combine egg white, vinegar, and pepper in a small bowl and whisk to blend. Very slowly drizzle in olive oil, whisking constantly until mixture is stiff. Measure 2 tablespoons mayonnaise; reserve remainder for another use.

Combine tuna, mayonnaise, scallions, Thai seasoning, sesame oil, and sesame seed in a mixing bowl and mix well.

Spread rice smoothly on nori, dividing evenly. Smear rice with wasabi. Top with layer of tuna mixture. Working with 1 roll at a time, hold seaweed with both hands and roll up slowly until ends meet. Drape a piece of plastic wrap over roll; top with bamboo sushi mat. Squeeze gently until roll holds together. Remove plastic and bamboo mat. Repeat steps to make 3 more rolls.

Dip a very sharp knife into cold water and let excess drip off. Cut each roll into 6 crosswise slices. Arrange on plates and garnish with pickled ginger. Serve with soy sauce dip.

CALIFORNIA ROLL

The only tricky steps to making sushi are cooking the rice and rolling it up. But—please forgive the mixed metaphor—you'll find my method of cooking Sushi Rice a piece of cake. Try it.

2 CUPS COOKED SUSHI RICE (SEE PAGE 114)

2 SHEETS NORI, CUT IN HALF

1 TABLESPOON WASABI POWDER MIXED WITH 1 TABLESPOON WARM WATER TO MAKE PASTE

8 OUNCES ALASKA KING CRAB MEAT

½ RIPE AVOCADO, CUT INTO 8 WEDGES

1 2-INCH PIECE CUCUMBER, PEELED, SEEDED, AND CUT INTO THIN LENGTHWISE STRIPS

2 TEASPOONS SESAME SEED

6 OUNCES PICKLED GINGER (GARNISH)

SOY SAUCE DIP (SEE PAGE 16)

Spread ¼ of the rice smoothly over a sheet of nori. Turn rice-side-down on cutting board. Smear nori with wasabi. Arrange ¼ of the crab, 2 avocado wedges, and ¼ of the cucumber strips lengthwise down center. Holding with both hands, slowly roll up until edges of seaweed meet and filling ingredients are enclosed in center. Drape a piece of plastic wrap over roll; top with bamboo sushi mat. Squeeze gently until roll holds together. Remove plastic and bamboo mat. Sprinkle roll with sesame seed. Repeat steps to make 3 more California rolls.

Dip a very sharp knife into cold water and let excess drip off. Cut each roll into 6 crosswise slices. Arrange on plates and serve with pickled ginger and soy sauce dip.

TIGER'S EYE

This dish is easy to prepare and absolutely beautiful. I promise that if you make it for guests it will knock their socks off.

4 PIECES SMOKED SALMON,
    4 X ½ INCHES

4 PIECES PEELED CUCUMBER,
    4 X ¼ INCHES

2 SHEETS NORI, CUT IN HALF

4 MEDIUM SQUID, CLEANED

SOY SAUCE DIP

¼ CUP SOY SAUCE

1 TABLESPOON THINLY SLICED
    SCALLIONS

1 TABLESPOON FRESH LEMON JUICE

1 TEASPOON TOMMY TANG'S THAI
    SEASONING

½ TEASPOON WASABI POWDER MIXED
    WITH ½ TEASPOON WARM WATER TO
    MAKE PASTE

Preheat oven to 450° F. Wrap 1 piece each of salmon and cucumber in a half sheet of nori; insert gently into opening in 1 squid. Repeat with remaining salmon, cucumber, and squid. Place the stuffed squid on an ungreased baking tray and bake 10 minutes. Slice each squid crosswise into 6 rings.

Combine all ingredients for soy sauce dip and divide among small individual bowls. Arrange squid on a platter and serve hot or at room temperature with pickled ginger and soy sauce dip.

Meekrob

Pine nuts are not ordinarily used in Thai cooking, but this is my own version of meekrob. I find the traditional recipes too sweet, and I don't care for the usual pickled garlic topping —so I substitute pine nuts for the pickled garlic, use Tamarind Juice to counter the sweetness of the sugar, and add shredded leeks for a refreshing finish.

3 CUPS VEGETABLE OIL (FOR DEEP FRYING)

2 OUNCES MEEKROB NOODLES

3 TABLESPOONS OLIVE OIL

8 MEDIUM SHRIMP (21 TO 25 PER POUND), SHELLED AND DEVEINED

6 TABLESPOONS TAMARIND JUICE (SEE PAGE 112)

3 TABLESPOONS RICE VINEGAR

2 TABLESPOONS SUGAR OR HONEY

1 ½ TABLESPOONS THAI FISH SAUCE

1 TEASPOON PAPRIKA

1 EGG, BEATEN

2 OUNCES BEAN SPROUTS

½ CUP SHREDDED LEEKS

4 SPRIGS CILANTRO

2 TABLESPOONS TOASTED PINE NUTS

Line a large bowl with paper towels.

Pour vegetable oil into a large saucepan and heat to 375° F. (To test oil, drop in a small piece of noodle. If it immediately puffs and enlarges, oil is ready.) Drop half the noodles into the hot oil; noodles should immediately puff. Remove noodles quickly (do not let them color) and transfer to paper-towel-lined bowl to drain. Repeat with remaining noodles.

Heat olive oil in a large skillet over high heat. Add shrimp and sauté 1 minute. Add tamarind juice, vinegar, sugar, fish sauce, and paprika, bring to boil, and stir constantly until mixture is syrupy. Reduce heat to medium, add egg, and stir briskly until blended. Let sauce cool to lukewarm.

Transfer sauce to a large bowl, add noodles, and toss to coat well. Arrange noodles on a platter and top with bean sprouts, leeks, and cilantro. Sprinkle with pine nuts and serve.

Chicken Sate with Peanut Sauce

Every Asian chef has his own version of peanut sauce. Since it's one of the most sought-after recipes at my restaurant and I'm a nice guy, let me present it to you right here. By the way, do the right thing—don't even think of using peanut butter.

MARINADE

½ CUP TOMMY TANG'S THAI SATE MARINADE

4 TABLESPOONS COCONUT MILK (SEE PAGE 112) OR HALF-AND-HALF

1½ TABLESPOONS THAI FISH SAUCE

1 TABLESPOON HONEY

2 CHICKEN BREASTS (7 TO 8 OUNCES EACH), SKINNED, BONED, AND CUT INTO 2 X 1¼ X ¼-INCH PIECES

PEANUT SAUCE

3 TABLESPOONS OLIVE OIL

½ TEASPOON PANANG CURRY PASTE

½ TEASPOON ROASTED CHILI PASTE

½ TEASPOON CURRY POWDER

½ TEASPOON PAPRIKA

½ CUP COCONUT MILK (SEE PAGE 112) OR HALF-AND-HALF

½ CUP FINELY GROUND UNSALTED PEANUTS

2 TABLESPOONS CHICKEN STOCK (SEE PAGE 110)

1 TABLESPOON THAI FISH SAUCE

1 TEASPOON FRESH LIME JUICE OR LEMON JUICE

2 TABLESPOONS PURE HONEY

FOR BASTING

3 TABLESPOONS COCONUT MILK (SEE PAGE 112)

Combine marinade ingredients in a medium bowl and whisk until blended. Add chicken pieces and toss gently until well coated. Thread 3 chicken pieces lengthwise on each of eight 9-inch bamboo skewers, covering skewers. Place in refrigerator container, cover, and refrigerate at least 3 hours, preferably overnight.

For peanut sauce, heat olive oil in a medium saucepan over high heat. Add curry paste, chili paste, curry powder, paprika, and 2 tablespoons coconut milk and cook, stirring constantly, 1 minute. Add remaining 6 tablespoons coconut milk, peanuts, chicken stock, fish sauce, lime juice, and honey and bring to boil, stirring constantly. Reduce heat to low and simmer sauce for 10 minutes, stirring every 2 minutes to prevent sticking. Transfer to a small bowl and set aside at room temperature.

Prepare charcoal grill. Remove skewers with chicken pieces from container, reserving marinade that has drained off. Stir 3 tablespoons coconut milk into marinade and use mixture as basting sauce. Grill sates, basting frequently, for 2 to 2½ minutes on each side or until chicken is lightly charred but not overcooked. Serve immediately with peanut sauce.

For the oven broiler, if charcoal grill is not available: Wrap bamboo skewers with aluminum foil, leaving only the chicken exposed, or use stainless steel skewers in place of bamboo. Preheat broiler to high, place chicken sate on baking tray, baste chicken with all of basting sauce, and cook for 3 to 4 minutes, until moist inside and lightly charred outside.

SUGGESTION: Test the broiler with a stick of chicken sate to determine how hot the broiler is, since broiler temperatures vary.

Mussel Sate with Ginger Cream Sauce

I stole the idea for these from chicken sates—because they make a unique, colorful dish that's amazingly easy to fix, and simply because I love them.

8 CUPS WATER

24 LARGE NEW ZEALAND OR BLACK MUSSELS, SCRUBBED AND DEBEARDED

3 TABLESPOONS OLIVE OIL

2 TABLESPOONS TOMMY TANG'S THAI SEASONING

GINGER CREAM SAUCE

2 TABLESPOONS UNSALTED BUTTER

2 TABLESPOONS OLIVE OIL

2 TABLESPOONS FINELY CHOPPED SHALLOTS

2 TABLESPOONS FINELY CHOPPED GARLIC

¼ CUP FINELY CHOPPED, PEELED FRESH GINGER

½ CUP DRY WHITE WINE

1 TABLESPOON THAI FISH SAUCE

2 TEASPOONS WHITE PEPPER

¾ CUP COCONUT MILK (SEE PAGE 112)

1 ¼ CUPS WHIPPING CREAM

1 TABLESPOON CURRY POWDER

Bring water to boil in a large stockpot over high heat. Add mussels, cover, and steam for 3 minutes. Transfer mussels to a colander and rinse with cold water. Carefully remove shells without tearing mussels, discarding any unopened mussels. Thread 3 mussels on each of eight 8-inch bamboo skewers.

Prepare charcoal grill. Coat mussels with olive oil and Thai seasoning. Grill until mussels are cooked through, about 2 minutes on each side. Remove from heat and keep warm. (If a charcoal grill is not available, use the oven broiler as described in recipe for Chicken Sate with Peanut Sauce, page 18.)

For sauce, melt butter with olive oil in a deep saucepan over high heat. Add shallots and garlic and sauté 2 minutes. Add ginger and sauté 2 minutes. Add wine, fish sauce, and white pepper and bring to boil, then reduce heat to medium and cook, stirring constantly for 3 minutes. Add coconut milk, increase heat to high, and bring to boil; boil 2 minutes. Stir in cream and return to boil. Reduce heat to low and simmer until reduced by half, about 5 minutes. Strain sauce through a fine sieve and keep warm.

Reserve 2 tablespoons sauce. Spread remainder on 4 serving plates, dividing it evenly. Place 2 mussel sates to 1 side of each plate. Combine reserved sauce with curry powder in a squeeze bottle and shake to blend well. Squeeze decorative lines or designs of curry accent into the sauce on each plate and serve.

Volcanic Mussels

The reason for the name of this dish will become apparent when you serve it: as the foil covering is opened, steam rushes out of the pot like an erupting volcano. Though simple to cook, these unusually seasoned mussels are almost as good as a free trip to Hawaii.

2 ½ POUNDS NEW ZEALAND OR BLACK
    MUSSELS, SCRUBBED AND
    DEBEARDED
¼ CUP DRY WHITE WINE
¾ CUP LEMON GRASS STOCK OR
    CHICKEN STOCK (SEE PAGE 110)
½ CUP TOMATO PUREE (SEE PAGE 111)
3 TABLESPOONS CHOPPED GARLIC
3 TABLESPOONS FINELY CHOPPED
    BASIL

2 TABLESPOONS CHOPPED TOMATOES
1 ½ TABLESPOONS THAI FISH SAUCE
2 SPRIGS FRESH OR DRIED LEMON
    GRASS, OR 1 TABLESPOON LEMON
    GRASS POWDER
2 TABLESPOONS UNSALTED BUTTER
1 TEASPOON WHITE PEPPER

Preheat oven to 350° F. Combine all ingredients in a stockpot or other deep ovenproof container. Wrap the whole pot tightly with 2 layers of aluminum foil and bake for 30 minutes.

Bring the stockpot to the table and place on a trivet or mat. Quickly slit top of foil with knife, allowing steam to escape. Serve at once, discarding any unopened mussels.

THAI EGG ROLLS

Egg rolls, egg rolls, egg rolls—Chinese egg rolls, Vietnamese egg rolls, Indo egg rolls, Japanese egg rolls, Thai egg rolls—everybody makes egg rolls. What are the differences? Well, one is the sauce. Who wants to settle for plain soy sauce, ketchup, and mustard when you can create a wonderful sauce with chili paste, plum sauce, paprika, and peanuts? On Easter Sunday, maybe we should make egg rolls for the kids instead of painting eggs; we'll call them American egg rolls.

MAKES 8

¼ CUP OLIVE OIL

1 ½ TEASPOONS FINELY CHOPPED
  GARLIC

1 CUP CHOPPED BAMBOO SHOOTS

¾ CUP CHOPPED SHIITAKE MUSHROOMS

¾ CUP CHOPPED ONIONS

¾ CUP CHOPPED CELERY

¾ CUP CHOPPED CABBAGE

2 TABLESPOONS THAI SWEET BLACK
  BEAN SAUCE

1 TABLESPOON THAI FISH SAUCE

1 TABLESPOON SOY SAUCE

1 ½ TEASPOONS TOMMY TANG'S THAI
  SEASONING

3 TABLESPOONS COLD WATER

1 TABLESPOON CORNSTARCH

8 EGG-ROLL OR SPRING-ROLL SKINS

3 CUPS VEGETABLE OIL (FOR DEEP
  FRYING)

SWEET/SOUR DIPPING SAUCE

½ CUP WATER

¼ CUP SUGAR

¼ CUP RICE VINEGAR

2 TABLESPOONS PLUM SAUCE

¼ TEASPOON PAPRIKA

⅛ TEASPOON SALT

⅛ TEASPOON FRESH CHILI PASTE

2 TABLESPOONS GROUND UNSALTED
  PEANUTS

Heat olive oil in a medium skillet over high heat. Add garlic and sauté until lightly colored, about 1 minute. Add bamboo shoots, mushrooms, onions, celery, and cabbage and stir-fry 2 minutes. Add bean sauce, fish sauce, soy sauce, and Thai seasoning and stir for 3 minutes. Remove from heat.

Line a large strainer with 4 folded paper towels. Transfer vegetable mixture to strainer and let stand in the sink or over a bowl until cooled; excess liquid will drain off.

Combine water and cornstarch in a small saucepan over low heat and cook, stirring constantly, until thick and clear, about 1 to 2 minutes. Set aside.

Place ⅛ of the stuffing mixture in a strip diagonally across an egg-roll skin, just off center; leave a 2-inch margin at each end. Fold up smaller half of skin to cover stuffing.

Fold in left and right sides to cover ends of stuffing. Spread larger half of egg-roll skin with cornstarch "glue," then continue rolling to completely enclose filling; press to seal. Repeat with remaining filling and skins.

Heat vegetable oil in a large saucepan to 350° F. Deep-fry egg rolls in batches until browned on all sides, about 3 to 4 minutes. Remove and drain on paper towels. Serve hot with dipping sauce.

To make sauce, combine all ingredients except peanuts in a small saucepan and bring to boil over high heat. Reduce heat to low and simmer 4 minutes. Remove from heat and let cool. Stir in peanuts. Turn into individual bowls.

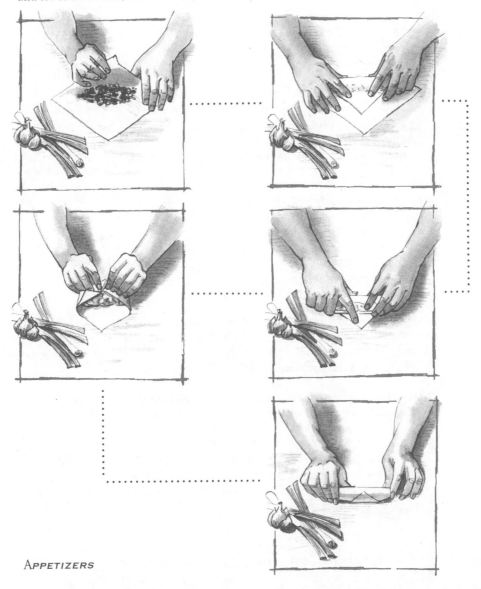

CRAB SPRING ROLLS WITH SANTA FE CHILI YOGURT SAUCE

So why don't I call these egg rolls? Well, "spring" sounds lighter than "egg," and this sauce is lighter and prettier than the egg-roll sauce, and anyway, why not?

MAKES 8

2 TABLESPOONS UNSALTED BUTTER

1½ TEASPOONS CHOPPED GARLIC

1 CUP FINELY DICED ONIONS

1 CUP FINELY DICED CARROTS

1 CUP FINELY DICED MUSHROOMS

2 TABLESPOONS FINELY CHOPPED CILANTRO

6 OUNCES SNOW, KING, OR BLUE CRAB MEAT

1 TABLESPOON THAI FISH SAUCE

1 TABLESPOON TOMMY TANG'S THAI SEASONING

1 TEASPOON WHITE PEPPER

3 TABLESPOONS COLD WATER

1 TABLESPOON CORNSTARCH

8 SPRING-ROLL OR EGG-ROLL SKINS

3 CUPS VEGETABLE OIL (FOR DEEP FRYING)

CHILI YOGURT SAUCE

½ CUP PLAIN LOW-FAT YOGURT

3 TABLESPOONS FINELY CHOPPED CILANTRO

1 TABLESPOON GRANULATED GARLIC

1½ TEASPOONS SANTA FE CHILI POWDER OR CAYENNE PEPPER

Melt butter in a skillet over medium heat. Add garlic and sauté until lightly colored, about 1½ minutes. Increase heat to high, add onions, carrots, mushrooms, and cilantro and stir-fry 2 minutes. Add crab, fish sauce, Thai seasoning, and pepper and cook, stirring, for 2 more minutes. Remove from heat and let cool.

Combine water and cornstarch in small saucepan over low heat and cook, stirring constantly, until thick and clear, about 1 to 2 minutes. Set aside.

Place ⅛ of the stuffing mixture in a strip along 1 side of a spring-roll skin, leaving margins at the ends. Fold up edge of skin just to cover stuffing. Fold in left and right sides to cover ends of stuffing. Spread top of egg-roll skin with cornstarch "glue," then continue rolling to completely enclose filling; press to seal. Repeat with remaining filling and skins.

Heat vegetable oil in a large saucepan to 350° F. Deep-fry spring rolls in batches until browned on all sides, about 3 to 4 minutes. Remove and drain on paper towels. Serve hot with chili yogurt sauce for dipping.

To make sauce, combine all ingredients in a mixing bowl and whisk until blended. Turn into individual bowls.

Thai Wonton

Okay, I admit it. I'm pirating a Chinese dish here, and I didn't pay royalties or a licensing fee. But centuries ago the Thai people actually were a hill tribe in China, and they migrated south only to get out of the way when war broke out between the Chinese and the Mongolians. So I hope this gets me off the hook for adopting wonton as my own.

MAKES 20

WONTON

3 OUNCES UNCOOKED SHRIMP, SHELLED, DEVEINED, AND MINCED OR GROUND

2 OUNCES UNCOOKED CHICKEN BREAST MEAT, MINCED OR GROUND

1 TABLESPOON FINELY CHOPPED CILANTRO

1 TABLESPOON DICED SCALLIONS

1½ TEASPOONS THAI FISH SAUCE

1 TEASPOON GRANULATED GARLIC

1 TEASPOON WHITE PEPPER

½ BEATEN EGG

20 WONTON WRAPPERS

3 CUPS VEGETABLE OIL (FOR DEEP FRYING)

SWEET/SOUR DIPPING SAUCE (SEE PAGE 22)

For wonton, combine shrimp, chicken, cilantro, scallions, fish sauce, garlic, pepper, and egg in a bowl and mix well with a fork. Place a small mound of filling mixture in the center of 1 wonton wrapper and fold in half diagonally to form a triangle. Dip a finger in cold water and wet wonton skin halfway between filling and 1 folded corner. Lift this corner and opposite corner over filling, overlap at moistened spot, and squeeze gently to seal. Repeat with remaining filling and wrappers.

Heat oil in a large saucepan to 350° F. Deep-fry wonton in batches until browned on all sides, about 2 minutes. Remove and drain on paper towels. Serve hot with dipping sauce.

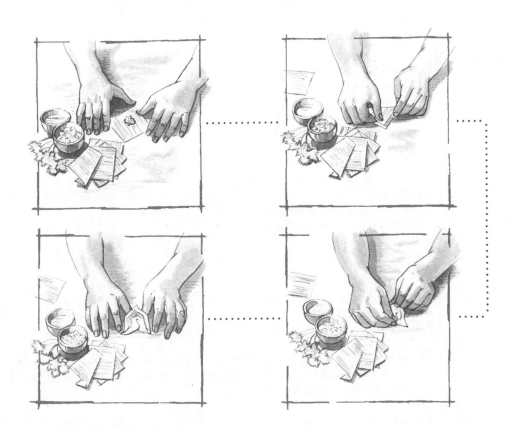

Spicy Wonton with Sweet Tamarind Sauce

Great for cocktail party finger food, these are simple to make, fun to serve, and very tasty.

MAKES 20

SWEET TAMARIND SAUCE

1 CUP TAMARIND JUICE (SEE PAGE 112)

¼ CUP SUGAR

½ TEASPOON FINELY CHOPPED SERRANO CHILI

¼ TEASPOON SALT

WONTON

2 TABLESPOONS UNSALTED BUTTER

1 TABLESPOON OLIVE OIL

6 OUNCES CHICKEN BREAST MEAT, GROUND

1 CUP FINELY CHOPPED, COOKED PEELED POTATOES

1 CUP PEAS, UNCOOKED

1 ½ TABLESPOONS THAI FISH SAUCE

1 TABLESPOON CURRY POWDER

1 TABLESPOON GRANULATED GARLIC

1 ½ TEASPOONS WHITE PEPPER

20 WONTON WRAPPERS

3 CUPS VEGETABLE OIL (FOR DEEP FRYING)

Combine all ingredients for sauce in a small saucepan and bring to a boil over high heat. Reduce heat to low and simmer until sauce is syrupy, about 8 to 10 minutes. Remove from heat and let cool. Turn into individual bowls and set aside.

For wonton, melt butter with olive oil in a skillet over high heat. Add chicken and sauté 4 minutes. Add all remaining filling ingredients and cook, stirring constantly, for 5 minutes. Remove from heat and let cool.

Place a tablespoonful of filling mixture on the center of 1 wonton wrapper. Wet edge of wrapper and fold in half diagonally to form a triangle. Gently press edges to seal. Repeat with remaining filling and wrappers.

Heat vegetable oil in a large saucepan to 350° F. Deep-fry wonton in batches until browned on all sides, about 2 minutes. Remove and drain on paper towels. Serve hot with sauce for dipping.

LARB

This dish originated in northeastern Thailand. Since there has been a great influx of people from that area into Bangkok, larb is now a big favorite there, too.

1 SMALL HEAD ROMAINE, GREEN-LEAF, OR ICEBERG LETTUCE

6 OUNCES BEEF FILLET OR CHICKEN BREAST MEAT, MINCED

2 TABLESPOONS LEMON GRASS STOCK OR CHICKEN STOCK (SEE PAGE 110)

3 TABLESPOONS DICED SCALLIONS

2 TABLESPOONS THAI FISH SAUCE

2 TABLESPOONS CHOPPED MINT LEAVES

2 TABLESPOONS FRESH LIME JUICE OR LEMON JUICE

1 TABLESPOON TOASTED RICE POWDER *

1 TEASPOON FINELY CHOPPED GARLIC

¼ TEASPOON CRUSHED RED PEPPER OR CAYENNE PEPPER

¼ TEASPOON SUGAR (OPTIONAL)

* TO PREPARE TOASTED RICE POWDER, PLACE ¼ CUP UNCOOKED WHITE RICE IN A SMALL SKILLET AND TOAST OVER MEDIUM HEAT UNTIL GOLDEN BROWN, ABOUT 6 MINUTES, STIRRING FREQUENTLY. REMOVE FROM HEAT AND LET COOL. TRANSFER RICE TO A BLENDER OR FOOD PROCESSOR AND GRIND TO POWDER. STORE EXTRA RICE POWDER IN AN AIRTIGHT CONTAINER; IT WILL KEEP INDEFINITELY.

Separate lettuce leaves; wash and dry. Arrange on a platter and set aside.

Combine meat and stock in a small saucepan and cook over high heat, stirring constantly, until meat is cooked through, 2 to 3 minutes. Remove from heat and stir in all remaining ingredients. Transfer meat mixture to a plate. To serve, have diners place a spoonful of filling onto each lettuce leaf and fold leaf over.

King Cobra

When I first tried this dish in Thailand, where it's called mieng-cum, an old man told me that it tastes like king cobra meat. (I took his word for it, since I can't say I'd be too eager to try the real thing.) I served this at the party celebrating the opening of my New York restaurant, and a guest asked what it was called. My mind went blank—I hadn't come up with a name yet. So I just answered "King Cobra." He thought it was a great name; I just smiled and said a silent thanks to that old man.

COCONUT CHILI SAUCE

2 TABLESPOONS UNSALTED BUTTER

¼ CUP PALM SUGAR OR HONEY

1 TEASPOON ROASTED CHILI PASTE

¼ CUP FLAKED COCONUT

½ CUP COCONUT MILK (SEE PAGE 112)

2 TABLESPOONS THAI FISH SAUCE

2 TABLESPOONS GROUND UNSALTED PEANUTS

2 HEADS BELGIAN ENDIVE OR INSIDE LEAVES OF 2 HEADS OF ROMAINE LETTUCE

TOPPING

6 OUNCES COOKED MEDIUM SHRIMP (21 TO 25 PER POUND), SHELLED, DEVEINED, AND CUT INTO ¼-INCH DICE

3 TABLESPOONS WHOLE, UNPEELED LIME CUT INTO ¼-INCH DICE

3 TABLESPOONS PEELED FRESH GINGER CUT INTO ¼-INCH DICE

3 TABLESPOONS SHALLOTS CUT INTO ¼-INCH DICE

3 TABLESPOONS FINELY DICED FRESH LEMON GRASS

2 TABLESPOONS FINELY DICED SERRANO CHILIES

½ CUP TOASTED COCONUT

2½ TABLESPOONS TOASTED PINE NUTS

For the sauce, melt butter in a small saucepan over medium heat. Add palm sugar and chili paste and stir until palm sugar is melted, about 2 minutes. Add flaked coconut, coconut milk, fish sauce, and ground peanuts and bring to boil. Reduce heat and simmer for 5 minutes, then remove from heat and let cool.

Separate endive leaves, wash and dry. Arrange on a platter.

Place topping ingredients in individual small bowls, or arrange ingredients in cobra design (see photo). To serve, have diners top each endive leaf with several pieces each of first 6 topping ingredients. Spoon on about 1 teaspoon sauce; sprinkle with coconut and pine nuts.

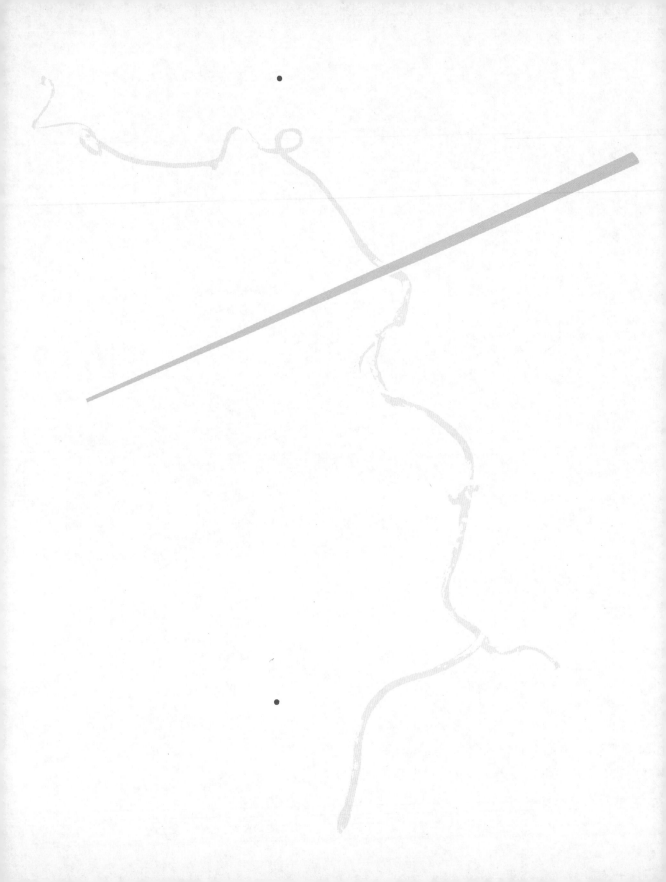

SOUPS AND SALADS

Tom Kha Kai

The Thai name of this soup literally means "boiled galanga chicken." It's one of the country's two favorite soups, and the combination of coconut milk, galanga, and lemon grass is truly memorable. Substitute shrimp and you have—you guessed it—Tom Kha Kung.

5 CUPS COCONUT MILK (SEE PAGE 112)

8 PIECES DRIED GALANGA OR
  1 TABLESPOON GALANGA POWDER

1 STALK LEMON GRASS OR 1 TEASPOON
  LEMON GRASS POWDER

2 TEASPOONS OLIVE OIL

1 TEASPOON CHOPPED GARLIC

8 OUNCES CHICKEN BREAST MEAT,
  DICED, OR 12 SHELLED, DEVEINED
  MEDIUM SHRIMP (21 TO 25 PER
  POUND)

½ CUP DICED MUSHROOMS

3 TABLESPOONS THAI FISH SAUCE

3 TABLESPOONS FRESH LIME JUICE

2 TEASPOONS ROASTED CHILI PASTE

2 TABLESPOONS DICED SCALLIONS

4 SPRIGS CILANTRO (LEAVES ONLY)

Combine coconut milk, galanga, and lemon grass in a medium saucepan and bring to boil over high heat. Reduce heat and simmer until reduced to 4 cups, about 22 to 25 minutes. Discard galanga and lemon grass.

Meanwhile, heat olive oil in a small skillet over medium heat. Add garlic and sauté until golden brown, about 1½ to 2 minutes. Add garlic to reduced soup along with chicken, mushrooms, fish sauce, lime juice, and chili paste and return to boil. Remove from heat and transfer to tureen or serving bowl. Sprinkle scallions and cilantro on top and serve.

Tom Yum Kung

When it's chilly out and you've caught a cold, nothing is more appealing than a hot bowl of this soup. The combination of lemon grass and mint is soothing and warming.

4 CUPS LEMON GRASS STOCK (SEE PAGE 110)

1 TEASPOON OLIVE OIL

½ TEASPOON SLICED GARLIC

12 SHELLED, DEVEINED MEDIUM SHRIMP (21 TO 25 PER POUND) OR 6 OUNCES DICED CHICKEN BREAST MEAT

½ CUP DICED MUSHROOMS

3 TABLESPOONS THAI FISH SAUCE

3 TABLESPOONS FRESH LIME JUICE

1 TABLESPOON ROASTED CHILI PASTE

⅓ CUP DICED TOMATOES

2 TABLESPOONS DICED SCALLIONS

16 SMALL MINT LEAVES

Bring lemon grass stock to boil in a medium saucepan over high heat, then reduce heat and keep at a simmer. Meanwhile, heat olive oil in a small skillet over medium heat. Add garlic and sauté until golden brown, about 1½ to 2 minutes. Add garlic to stock with shrimp, mushrooms, fish sauce, lime juice, and chili paste and return to boil. Remove from heat and transfer to a tureen or serving bowl. Add tomatoes, scallions, and mint and serve.

Arugula Salad with Rosemary Honey Vinaigrette

One hot day during the summer of 1986 I was strolling through Union Square Park in Manhattan, which in season becomes a farmer's market. I stopped at one of the produce stalls to admire a beautiful basket of arugula, whose fresh green leaves have a flavor that reminds me of almonds and pine nuts. I wanted to create a cooling, refreshing dish with the arugula, and this is it.

ROSEMARY HONEY VINAIGRETTE

½ CUP OLIVE OIL

3 CLOVES GARLIC, THINLY SLICED

6 TABLESPOONS WHITE ZINFANDEL

3 TABLESPOONS HONEY

2 TABLESPOONS SOY SAUCE

2 TEASPOONS GRATED, PEELED FRESH GINGER

2 CLOVES GARLIC, FINELY CHOPPED

1 TEASPOON POWDERED ROSEMARY

½ TEASPOON WHITE PEPPER

½ TEASPOON SALT

¼ CUP FRESH LEMON JUICE

6 BUNCHES ARUGULA, WASHED, DRIED, AND TRIMMED

1 ROASTED RED BELL PEPPER,* CUT INTO ¼-INCH LENGTHWISE STRIPS

6 SUN-DRIED TOMATOES PACKED IN OIL, DRAINED AND CUT INTO ¼-INCH SLICES

* TO ROAST BELL PEPPER, SEE RECIPE FOR RED BELL PEPPER PUREE, PAGE 111.

Heat olive oil in a small skillet over medium heat. Add sliced garlic and sauté until crisp and golden brown, 1½ to 2 minutes. Lift out garlic with a slotted spoon and drain on paper towels; set aside. Let oil cool.

In a large bowl, combine cooled oil with all remaining vinaigrette ingredients except lemon juice; whisk to blend. Slowly drizzle in lemon juice, whisking constantly.

Add arugula to vinaigrette and toss lightly to coat. Transfer arugula to platter or large salad bowl. Add red pepper and tomato slices to vinaigrette remaining in bowl and toss; sprinkle over arugula. Top with reserved sautéed garlic and serve.

THAI SAUSAGE SALAD

Thai and Chinese sausage are similar. Some are made with pork, some with liver and pork; they can be very fatty, regular, or extra-lean. I prefer to use the extra-lean type. Try this sausage with a hot dog bun; you'll love it.

4 THAI SAUSAGES

6 TABLESPOONS OLIVE OIL
1 ½ TEASPOONS CHOPPED GARLIC

3 TABLESPOONS THAI FISH SAUCE
3 TABLESPOONS FRESH LIME JUICE
1 TABLESPOON HONEY
¾ CUP DICED TOMATOES
⅓ CUP SLICED ONIONS
⅓ CUP JULIENNED CUCUMBER (PEELED AND SEEDED)
1 SMALL HEAD ROMAINE LETTUCE, WASHED, DRIED, AND CUT INTO BITE-SIZE PIECES

1 SMALL HEAD RADICCHIO, WASHED, DRIED, AND CUT INTO BITE-SIZE PIECES
3 TABLESPOONS THINLY SLICED, PEELED FRESH GINGER
2 TABLESPOONS DICED SCALLIONS
2 TABLESPOONS CHOPPED CILANTRO
½ TEASPOON FINELY CHOPPED SERRANO CHILI

4 SPRIGS CILANTRO (GARNISH)

Bring 2 inches of water to boil in a medium saucepan. Add sausages and simmer 10 minutes. Remove and pat dry with paper towels. Transfer sausage to a medium skillet and cook over medium heat, turning frequently, until browned on all sides, about 6 to 8 minutes. Drain on paper towels. Cut sausages diagonally into ⅛-inch-thick slices about 2 inches long. Set aside.

Heat olive oil in a small skillet over medium heat. Add garlic and sauté until golden brown, 1½ to 2 minutes. Remove from heat and let cool.

Combine cooled oil and garlic, fish sauce, lime juice, and honey in a large bowl and whisk until thick and emulsified. Add all remaining ingredients except the sausage and cilantro garnish and toss gently to coat. Lift salad out and transfer to a serving bowl. Toss sausage with dressing remaining in mixing bowl, arrange over salad. Garnish with cilantro sprigs and serve.

Warm Spinach-Chicken Salad

I used to be addicted to warm spinach salad—it's served in every restaurant. After finally OD'ing, I sought help from spinach AA. They advised me to drop the cooked egg and bacon bits, and replace them with marinated chicken. I've been sober ever since.

MARINADE

1 TABLESPOON OLIVE OIL

1 TEASPOON FINELY CHOPPED GARLIC

½ TEASPOON THAI FISH SAUCE

½ TEASPOON CORNSTARCH

¼ TEASPOON THAI SWEET BLACK BEAN SAUCE

¼ TEASPOON WHITE PEPPER

5 OUNCES CHICKEN BREAST MEAT, SLICED

1 BUNCH FRESH SPINACH, WASHED, DRIED, AND STEMMED

½ CUP THINLY SLICED RED ONIONS

½ CUP SLICED MUSHROOMS

½ CUP OLIVE OIL

1 TABLESPOON CHOPPED GARLIC

1 TEASPOON BLACK PEPPER

¼ CUP RICE VINEGAR

¼ CUP DRY WHITE WINE

2 TABLESPOONS SOY SAUCE

Combine marinade ingredients in a small bowl.

Add chicken and rub gently with marinade. Cover with plastic wrap and refrigerate 3 hours. Place spinach in a large salad bowl, arrange sliced onions and mushrooms in a circle on top.

Heat olive oil in a small saucepan over high heat. Add garlic and sauté until lightly colored, about 1½ minutes. Add chicken and pepper and sauté, stirring constantly, for 3 minutes. Stir in remaining ingredients and bring to boil; boil 1 minute. Pour chicken and dressing onto salad and serve.

Mango Salsa

I've been told that "salsa" sounds too Mexican for a Thai cookbook, but actually Mexican and Thai cuisines have quite a few ingredients in common—lime juice, tomatoes, serrano chilies, cilantro, and so on. Eat this plain as a side dish, or scoop it onto lettuce or cabbage leaves for a salad or appetizer. It also makes a great combination with scallops; see the recipe on page 97. If you can't find green mango anywhere, substitute tart green apple.

2 TABLESPOONS SUGARCANE JUICE OR
   1½ TABLESPOONS HONEY OR PALM
   SUGAR

¼ CUP THAI FISH SAUCE

¼ CUP FRESH LIME JUICE

½ TEASPOON ROASTED CHILI PASTE

6 OUNCES GREEN MANGO, PEELED,
   SEEDED, AND DICED (1½ CUPS)

⅓ CUP DICED SEEDED TOMATOES

3 TABLESPOONS DICED SCALLIONS

2 TABLESPOONS THINLY SLICED
   SHALLOTS

2 TABLESPOONS FINELY CHOPPED
   CILANTRO

2 TABLESPOONS THINLY SLICED FRESH
   LEMON GRASS

1 TEASPOON FINELY CHOPPED GARLIC

1 TEASPOON FINELY CHOPPED
   SERRANO CHILI

4 SPRIGS CILANTRO (GARNISH)

Combine sugarcane juice, fish sauce, lime juice, and chili paste in a large bowl and whisk until well blended. Add all remaining ingredients except cilantro garnish and toss until completely coated. Transfer to a serving bowl and garnish with cilantro.

Thai Papaya Salad

Pungent chili, tart lime juice, and refreshing fruit combine to create the best salad I've ever tasted, and by far the most popular one in Thailand. Known as som tum or "mashed melon," this can be found on every street corner and canal boat in the country. Each province has its own version. I've traveled all over hoping to find the best, but it's impossible to pick one—how do you choose the most perfect of the perfect?

5 TABLESPOONS FRESH LIME JUICE

¼ CUP THAI FISH SAUCE

2 TABLESPOONS SHRIMP POWDER

1 ½ TABLESPOONS PALM SUGAR OR HONEY

1 TEASPOON FINELY CHOPPED GARLIC

1 TEASPOON FINELY CHOPPED SERRANO CHILI

6 OUNCES GREEN PAPAYA, PEELED, SEEDED, AND SHREDDED IN A FOOD PROCESSOR (ABOUT 2 CUPS)

⅓ CUP GREEN BEANS CUT INTO 1-INCH LENGTHS

⅓ CUP DICED TOMATOES

3 TABLESPOONS GROUND UNSALTED PEANUTS

2 TABLESPOONS CHOPPED CILANTRO

4 SPRIGS CILANTRO (GARNISH)

Combine lime juice, fish sauce, shrimp powder, palm sugar, garlic, and chili in a large bowl and whisk until well blended. Add remaining ingredients except garnish and toss until completely coated. Using a small wooden mallet or an empty wine bottle, gently pound ingredients for about a minute to soften papaya. Transfer salad to platter, garnish with cilantro, and serve.

Eat this plain or scoop it onto lettuce or cabbage leaves for a salad appetizer.

Naked Shrimp Salad

I don't know what state of mind I was in when I named this dish, but just calling it "shrimp salad" is too simple. I guess the idea of undressing the shrimp makes them sound sexier and more appetizing. But don't daydream, now; these are, after all, just shrimp.

16 MEDIUM SHRIMP (21 TO 25 PER POUND), SHELLED AND DEVEINED

2 TABLESPOONS OLIVE OIL

1 TABLESPOON TOMMY TANG'S THAI SEASONING

¼ CUP VIRGIN OLIVE OIL

2 TABLESPOONS THAI FISH SAUCE

2 TABLESPOONS FRESH LIME JUICE OR LEMON JUICE

1½ TEASPOONS HONEY

1½ TEASPOONS ROASTED CHILI PASTE

1 TEASPOON FINELY CHOPPED GARLIC

1 TEASPOON FINELY CHOPPED SERRANO CHILI

1 SMALL HEAD ROMAINE LETTUCE, WASHED, DRIED AND CUT INTO BITE-SIZE PIECES

1 HEAD RADICCHIO, WASHED, DRIED, AND CUT INTO BITE-SIZE PIECES

⅓ CUP JULIENNED (PEELED AND SEEDED) CUCUMBER

2 TABLESPOONS CHOPPED MINT LEAVES

4 SPRIGS MINT (GARNISH)

Prepare charcoal grill if using. Coat shrimp with olive oil and Thai seasoning in a small bowl. Grill or cook in a large skillet over high heat until opaque, about 3 minutes on each side. Remove from heat and set aside.

Combine virgin olive oil, fish sauce, lime juice, honey, chili paste, garlic, and chopped chili in a large bowl and whisk until emulsified. Add lettuce, radicchio, cucumber, and chopped mint and toss gently until completely coated with dressing. Transfer vegetables to a platter. Add shrimp to dressing remaining in bowl and stir until dressing is absorbed. Arrange shrimp over vegetables, garnish with mint, and serve.

Spicy Beef Salad with Lemon Grass Sauce

You might come across a similar salad in a restaurant that serves nouvelle French or California cuisine. But don't be misled as to the origin of the recipe. I'll give you a hint . . . it's a country whose name starts with T.

12 OUNCES BEEF FILLET, ½ INCH THICK

2 TABLESPOONS OLIVE OIL

2 TEASPOONS TOMMY TANG'S THAI SEASONING

6 TABLESPOONS VIRGIN OLIVE OIL

3 TABLESPOONS THAI FISH SAUCE

3 TABLESPOONS FRESH LIME JUICE OR LEMON JUICE

1 TABLESPOON HONEY

1 TABLESPOON THINLY SLICED FRESH LEMON GRASS

1 ½ TEASPOONS FINELY CHOPPED GARLIC

1 TEASPOON FINELY CHOPPED SERRANO CHILI

1 SMALL HEAD ROMAINE LETTUCE, WASHED, DRIED, AND CUT INTO BITE-SIZE PIECES

1 SMALL HEAD RADICCHIO, WASHED, DRIED, AND CUT INTO BITE-SIZE PIECES

1 SMALL BELGIAN ENDIVE, CUT INTO BITE-SIZE PIECES

⅓ CUP DICED TOMATOES

2 ROASTED ANAHEIM CHILIES,* CUT INTO BITE-SIZE PIECES

2 TABLESPOONS FINELY CHOPPED MINT LEAVES

1 SPRIG MINT (GARNISH)

* TO ROAST CHILIES, FOLLOW INSTRUCTIONS FOR ROASTING BELL PEPPERS IN RECIPE FOR RED BELL PEPPER PUREE, PAGE 111.

Prepare charcoal grill, if using. Coat beef thoroughly with olive oil and Thai seasoning. Grill for 4 minutes on each side, or cook in a nonstick skillet over high heat for 3 minutes on each side. Remove fillet from heat and slice thinly; set aside.

Combine virgin olive oil, fish sauce, lime juice, honey, lemon grass, garlic, and serrano chili in a large bowl and whisk until thick. Add remaining ingredients except garnish and toss gently to coat. Lift out vegetable mixture and transfer to a platter. Add beef to sauce remaining in bowl and toss until sauce is absorbed. Arrange beef over vegetables, garnish with mint sprig, and serve.

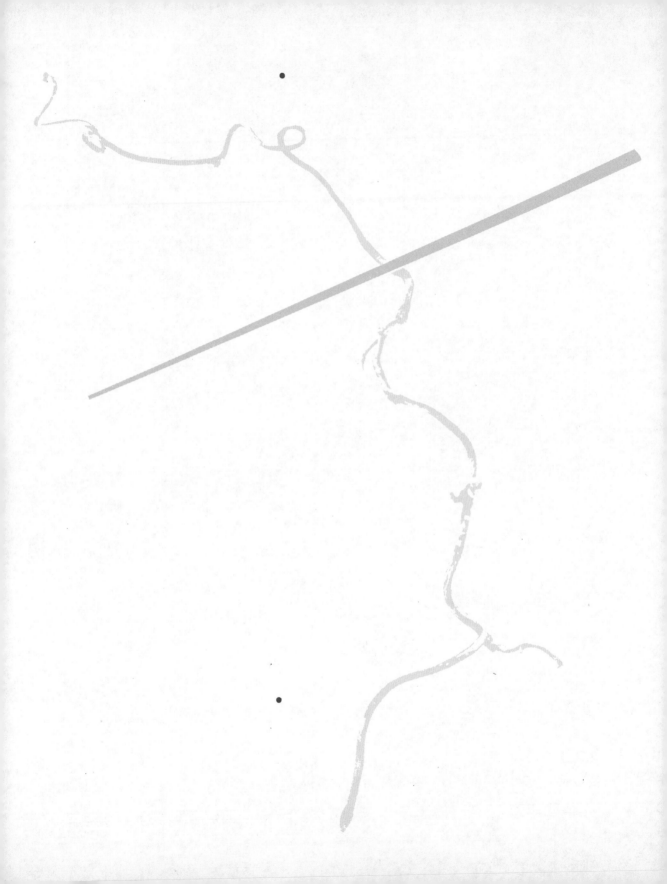

VEGETABLES

THAI EGGPLANT

A twist on the basic Thai recipe for this dish; as far as I know, we're the only ones who use olive oil and pine nuts.

½ CUP OLIVE OIL

2 TABLESPOONS FINELY CHOPPED RED ONIONS

2 TABLESPOONS FINELY CHOPPED GARLIC

1 POUND ASIAN OR REGULAR UNPEELED EGGPLANT, THINLY SLICED

6 TABLESPOONS TOASTED PINE NUTS

8 SMALL DRIED CHILIES

3 TABLESPOONS CHICKEN STOCK (SEE PAGE 110)

2 TABLESPOONS THAI SWEET BLACK BEAN SAUCE

1 TABLESPOON ROASTED CHILI PASTE

¼ CUP CHOPPED THAI OR REGULAR BASIL

1 TEASPOON BLACK PEPPER

2 SPRIGS BASIL (GARNISH)

Heat oil in a large skillet over high heat. Add onions and garlic and sauté until garlic is lightly colored. Add eggplant and sauté 1 minute. Add remaining ingredients except garnish and cook, stirring constantly, until eggplant is tender, about 4 to 5 minutes. Transfer to a platter, garnish with basil, and serve.

SPINACH WITH BLACK BEAN SAUCE

Plain steamed spinach is not what I'd call an exciting dish. But this combination . . . well, you'll find it quite a different story.

6 CUPS HOT WATER

2 BUNCHES FRESH SPINACH, WASHED, DRIED, AND STEMMED

6 TABLESPOONS OLIVE OIL

1 ½ TEASPOONS FINELY CHOPPED GARLIC

2 TABLESPOONS THINLY SLICED, PEELED FRESH GINGER

2 TABLESPOONS SOY SAUCE

2 TEASPOONS THAI OR CHINESE BEAN CONDIMENT

2 TEASPOONS THAI SWEET BLACK BEAN SAUCE

½ TEASPOON BLACK PEPPER

Bring water to boil in a stockpot. Add spinach and boil just until wilted—it will be less than a minute. Drain spinach in a colander and set aside.

Heat oil in a large skillet over high heat. Add garlic and sauté until lightly colored. Add remaining ingredients and cook, stirring, for 1 minute. Add spinach and stir for 2 minutes. Transfer to a platter and serve.

MIXED VEGGIES

Great for emptying out the vegetable crisper, especially when you have odds and ends of different veggies but not enough to make any one dish. I do this often, since I'm a vegetable lover—and by adding some rice or pasta I have a flavorful meal for next to nothing.

3 TABLESPOONS OLIVE OIL

1 TEASPOON FINELY CHOPPED GARLIC

2 CUPS MIXED FRESH VEGETABLES CUT INTO BITE-SIZE PIECES

1 TABLESPOON THINLY SLICED, PEELED FRESH GINGER

1 TABLESPOON OYSTER SAUCE

2 TEASPOONS THAI FISH SAUCE

1 TEASPOON THAI SWEET BLACK BEAN SAUCE

1 TEASPOON TOMMY TANG'S THAI SEASONING

2 TABLESPOONS CHICKEN STOCK (SEE PAGE 110)

Heat oil in a medium skillet over high heat. Add garlic and sauté briefly. Add all remaining ingredients except chicken stock and stir-fry 2 minutes. Add stock and stir for 1 minute longer. Serve hot.

1. CHINESE CHIVE FLOWER
2. THAI EGGPLANT
3. THAI RED BASIL
4. THAI HOLY BASIL
5. ENOKI MUSHROOM
6. ROSEMARY
7. CILANTRO
8. MINT
9. FRESH TURMERIC ROOTS
10. KAFFIR LIME
11. KAFFIR LIME LEAF
12. FRESH GINGERROOT
13. THAI HOTTEST CHILI
14. THAI GREEN EGGPLANT
15. DAIKON SPROUT
16. LEMON GRASS
17. THAI GRAPE EGGPLANT

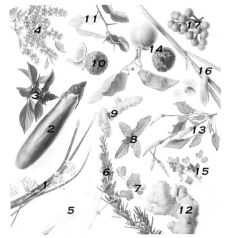

TIGER'S EYE [p. 16]

MEEKROB [p. 17]

PAD THAI [p. 56]

KING COBRA [p. 30]

THAI PASTA [p. 54]

THAI PAPAYA SALAD [p. 40] • BLACK OLIVE FRIED RICE [p. 69]

SHRIMP PANANG [*p. 74*]

Broccoli with Garlic Oyster Sauce

This dish had been on the menu in my restaurants for so long that I almost deleted it—until my wife Sandi became pregnant and the doctor told her to eat more calcium-rich foods. Broccoli came right back into the limelight.

6 CUPS HOT WATER

14 OUNCES BROCCOLI FLORETS (ABOUT 2 POUNDS BEFORE TRIMMING)

6 TABLESPOONS OLIVE OIL

1 ½ TEASPOONS FINELY CHOPPED GARLIC

½ CUP DICED MUSHROOMS

3 TABLESPOONS OYSTER SAUCE

2 TABLESPOONS CHICKEN STOCK (SEE PAGE 110)

2 TABLESPOONS THINLY SLICED, PEELED FRESH GINGER

2 TEASPOONS THAI SWEET BLACK BEAN SAUCE

½ TEASPOON BLACK PEPPER

Bring water to boil in a stockpot. Add broccoli and boil 2 minutes. Drain in a colander and set aside.

Heat oil in a large skillet over high heat. Add garlic and sauté until lightly colored. Add remaining ingredients and sauté 1 minute. Add broccoli and cook, stirring constantly, for 2 minutes to coat with sauce. Transfer to a serving bowl and serve at once.

Spicy Garlic Mushrooms

Not hallucinogenic, but you can still get a high from this combination. And did you know that spicy food makes you a better lover! But go easy on the chilies—otherwise your loved one may wind up embracing a Thai beer instead of you.

6 CUPS HOT WATER

10 OUNCES LARGE MUSHROOMS, TRIMMED

¼ CUP OLIVE OIL

6 TABLESPOONS FINELY CHOPPED RED ONIONS

3 TABLESPOONS FINELY CHOPPED GARLIC

1 TEASPOON FINELY CHOPPED SERRANO CHILI

1 TEASPOON ROASTED CHILI PASTE

¼ CUP RED BELL PEPPER PUREE (SEE PAGE 111)

¼ CUP LEMON GRASS STOCK OR CHICKEN STOCK (SEE PAGE 110)

2 TABLESPOONS THAI FISH SAUCE

1 TABLESPOON MAGGI SAUCE (OPTIONAL)

1 ½ TEASPOONS THAI SWEET BLACK BEAN SAUCE

1 TEASPOON FRESHLY GROUND BLACK PEPPER

2 TABLESPOONS FINELY DICED RED BELL PEPPER (GARNISH)

Bring water to boil in a medium stockpot. Add mushrooms and boil 2 minutes. Drain in a colander and set aside.

Heat oil in a large skillet over high heat. Add onions and garlic and sauté until browned, about 2 minutes. Add serrano chili and chili paste and sauté 1 minute. Add mushrooms and all remaining ingredients except garnish and cook, stirring constantly, until sauce is thickened, about 3 more minutes. Transfer to a platter, garnish with diced pepper, and serve.

BRUNEI EGG CREPES

One night the Sultan of Brunei and his entourage came into the restaurant for dinner. He sent his right-hand man into the kitchen to ask for an onion omelet. I remember answering, "An omelet? That's too simple!" So here's what I made; if it's good enough for a sultan it's good enough for you, too. I wish I knew how to say bon appetit in Arabic.

FILLING
2 TABLESPOONS OLIVE OIL
1 TEASPOON FINELY CHOPPED GARLIC
¼ CUP DICED ONIONS
¼ CUP DICED TOMATOES
¼ CUP DICED CELERY
¼ CUP DICED MUSHROOMS
3 TABLESPOONS DICED SCALLIONS
1½ TEASPOONS THAI FISH SAUCE
1½ TEASPOONS TOMMY TANG'S THAI SEASONING

1 TEASPOON THAI SWEET BLACK BEAN SAUCE

CREPES
4 LARGE EGGS
2 TABLESPOONS COLD WATER
1 TABLESPOON THAI FISH SAUCE
6 TABLESPOONS OLIVE OIL

2 SPRIGS CILANTRO (GARNISH)

For the filling, heat olive oil in a medium skillet over high heat. Add garlic and sauté until lightly browned, about 1 minute. Add onions, tomatoes, celery, mushrooms, scallions, fish sauce, Thai seasoning, and black bean sauce and cook, stirring constantly, 3 minutes. Set filling aside.

For the crepes, combine eggs, water, and fish sauce in a small bowl and whisk to blend well. Heat olive oil in a large nonstick skillet over high heat until extremely hot, about 2 minutes. Pour half the hot oil into a cup and reserve for second crepe. Pour half of the egg batter into the skillet and swirl to cover entire bottom. Reduce heat to low.

Place half the filling mixture in center of crepe and fold in all 4 sides to make a square. Place serving plate over skillet and invert crepe onto plate. Pour reserved oil back into skillet and reheat over high heat. Repeat procedure to make another filled crepe; invert onto second plate. Garnish each crepe with cilantro and serve.

NOODLES AND RICE

THAI PASTA

The debate goes on—who invented pasta, the Chinese or the Italians? Who cares, as long as it's good? So let's assume Marco Polo did learn how to make pasta in China. He must have been a good chef; look at all the great pasta dishes he invented. Suppose he'd learned how to do Peking duck . . . that's what we'd be eating in Italian restaurants today.

8 CUPS WATER

1 LARGE CHICKEN BREAST (7 TO
9 OUNCES), WITH SKIN AND BONE

1½ TEASPOONS VEGETABLE OIL
¼ TEASPOON SALT
12 OUNCES FRESH SPINACH PASTA
8 CUPS ICE WATER

¼ CUP OLIVE OIL
4 TEASPOONS CHOPPED GARLIC

¼ CUP FRESH LIME JUICE OR LEMON
JUICE
2 TABLESPOONS THAI FISH SAUCE

2 TABLESPOONS THAI SWEET BLACK
BEAN SAUCE
½ CUP SLICED RED ONIONS
½ CUP JULIENNED CARROTS
2 TABLESPOONS DICED SCALLIONS
½ TEASPOON DRIED OREGANO,
CRUSHED
½ TEASPOON CRUSHED RED PEPPER OR
CAYENNE PEPPER
½ TEASPOON BLACK PEPPER

¼ CUP FINELY DICED TOMATOES
(GARNISH)
4 SPRIGS CILANTRO (GARNISH)

Bring water to boil in a large saucepan. Add chicken breast and simmer 10 minutes. Remove chicken; discard skin and bone. Shred meat and set aside.

Add vegetable oil and salt to chicken cooking liquid and return to boil. Drop in pasta and boil until al dente, about 2 minutes. Drain, then drop into bowl of ice water. Drain well and set aside.

Heat olive oil in a small skillet over low heat. Add garlic and stir until lightly browned. Pour mixture into large mixing bowl and let cool.

Add reserved pasta, lime juice, fish sauce, black bean sauce, onions, carrots, scallions, oregano, red pepper, and black pepper to garlic mixture and toss until pasta is well coated. Transfer pasta to a platter, leaving excess dressing in bowl. Add reserved chicken to bowl and toss until remaining dressing is absorbed. Place chicken on pasta, garnish with tomatoes and cilantro, and serve.

Panang Curry Pasta with Pine Nuts and Basil

After Thai cooking, Italian is my second favorite. I invented this dish as a quick fix for my pasta habit—and to show how versatile Thai food can be.

8 CUPS WATER

1 ½ TEASPOONS VEGETABLE OIL

¼ TEASPOON SALT

12 OUNCES PENNE PASTA

3 TABLESPOONS OLIVE OIL

2 TABLESPOONS FINELY CHOPPED RED ONIONS

1 TABLESPOON FINELY CHOPPED GARLIC

1 TABLESPOON PANANG CURRY PASTE

1 CUP COCONUT MILK (SEE PAGE 112)

1 ½ TABLESPOONS THAI FISH SAUCE

2 TEASPOONS PAPRIKA

½ CUP WHIPPING CREAM

⅔ CUP SLICED SNOW PEAS

½ CUP THINLY SLICED RED BELL PEPPER

2 TABLESPOONS TOASTED PINE NUTS

2 TABLESPOONS CHOPPED FRESH BASIL

Bring water to boil in a stockpot with vegetable oil and salt. Add pasta and boil until al dente, about 7 minutes. Drain, rinse with cold water, and set aside.

Heat olive oil in a large skillet over medium heat. Add onions and garlic and sauté until lightly browned. Add curry paste and stir 1 minute. Add coconut milk, fish sauce, and paprika and bring to boil. Pour in cream, return to boil, and stir constantly for 2 minutes, then reduce heat to low and simmer 5 minutes. Add snow peas, bell pepper, pine nuts, basil, and reserved cooked pasta; toss to coat pasta well. Remove from heat, divide pasta among 4 dishes, and serve.

Pad Thai

This is Thailand's most famous noodle dish, something we enjoy morning, noon, and night. No matter where you go—sidewalks, temple festivals, floating markets—you'll find a vendor selling one or another version of pad thai.

12 OUNCES PAD THAI (SEN CHAN)
   NOODLES

8 CUPS COLD WATER

¼ CUP OLIVE OIL

1 TABLESPOON CHOPPED GARLIC

16 MEDIUM SHRIMP (21 TO 25 PER
   POUND), SHELLED AND DEVEINED

2 OUNCES FIRM BROWN TOFU, CUT INTO
   ¼-INCH DICE

2 EGGS, BEATEN

½ CUP TAMARIND JUICE (SEE
   PAGE 112)

¼ CUP CRUSHED UNSALTED PEANUTS

3 TABLESPOONS THAI FISH SAUCE

2½ TABLESPOONS RICE VINEGAR

1 TABLESPOON SUGAR OR
1½ TABLESPOONS HONEY

2 TEASPOONS PAPRIKA

½ TEASPOON CRUSHED RED PEPPER OR
   CAYENNE PEPPER

3 OUNCES FRESH BEAN SPROUTS

¼ CUP LEEKS CUT INTO 1½- TO 2-INCH-
   LONG SHREDS

In a large bowl, soak noodles in cold water 45 minutes. Drain in a colander and set aside.

Heat olive oil in a large skillet over high heat. Add garlic and sauté until lightly browned, about 1 minute. Add shrimp and tofu and sauté 1 minute. Add eggs and stir 30 seconds. Add reserved noodles, tamarind juice, peanuts, fish sauce, vinegar, sugar, paprika, and red pepper and stir constantly 3 minutes. Remove from heat and transfer to a platter. Sprinkle with bean sprouts and leeks and serve.

SANTA FE CHILI PASTA

When my friend Andy first visited my restaurant he requested a special pasta with cream sauce, so I invented this for him. I promised that I'd put the recipe in a cookbook so his lovely wife Donna won't have to dial (213) 651-1810 for takeout every time he craves it.

8 CUPS WATER

1 ½ TEASPOONS VEGETABLE OIL

¼ TEASPOON SALT

12 OUNCES PENNE PASTA

3 TABLESPOONS OLIVE OIL

2 TABLESPOONS FINELY CHOPPED RED ONIONS

1 TABLESPOON FINELY CHOPPED GARLIC

1 TABLESPOON SANTA FE CHILI POWDER

2 TEASPOONS ROASTED CHILI PASTE

1 CUP COCONUT MILK (SEE PAGE 112)

1 ½ TABLESPOONS THAI FISH SAUCE

1 CUP WHIPPING CREAM

4 SUN-DRIED TOMATOES, PACKED IN OIL, DRAINED AND CUT INTO ¼-INCH STRIPS

4 SPRIGS BASIL (GARNISH)

Bring water to boil in a stockpot with vegetable oil and salt. Add pasta and boil until al dente, about 7 minutes. Drain and set aside.

Heat olive oil in a heavy saucepan over high heat. Add onion and garlic and stir until lightly browned, about 2 minutes. Add chili powder and roasted chili paste and stir 1 minute. Add coconut milk and fish sauce and bring to boil; add cream and return to boil. Reduce heat to low and simmer 5 minutes, stirring every minute. Increase heat to medium, add cooked pasta, and stir until well coated with sauce. Transfer to a platter and top with sun-dried tomatoes. Garnish with basil and serve.

Lard-na Noodles

Lard-na *means "pour over your face"—but it really refers to pouring the savory sauce over a bed of noodles. After pad thai, this is Thailand's most popular noodle dish. I've searched all over the country to find the best lard-na, and I think Bangkok's version is the winner.*

1 TABLESPOON OLIVE OIL

1 ¼ POUNDS FRESH RICE NOODLES, CUT INTO 1-INCH-WIDE STRIPS

1 TEASPOON THAI FISH SAUCE

1 TEASPOON THAI SWEET BLACK BEAN SAUCE

2 TABLESPOONS OLIVE OIL

16 MEDIUM SHRIMP (21 TO 25 PER POUND), SHELLED AND DEVEINED, OR 8 OUNCES SLICED UNCOOKED BEEF, CHICKEN, OR PORK

12 OUNCES BROCCOLI FLORETS (ABOUT 1 ¾ POUNDS BEFORE TRIMMING)

1 ½ TEASPOONS FINELY CHOPPED GARLIC

2 TEASPOONS THAI OR CHINESE BEAN CONDIMENT

3 CUPS CHICKEN STOCK (SEE PAGE 110)

2 TABLESPOONS THAI FISH SAUCE

2 TABLESPOONS OYSTER SAUCE

1 TABLESPOON RICE VINEGAR

1 TEASPOON WHITE PEPPER

½ TEASPOON CRUSHED RED PEPPER OR CAYENNE PEPPER

1 ½ TABLESPOONS ALL-PURPOSE FLOUR MIXED WITH ¼ CUP COLD WATER

Heat 1 tablespoon olive oil in a large skillet over high heat. Add noodles and sauté 2 minutes. Add 1 teaspoon fish sauce and black bean sauce and sauté 1 minute longer. Transfer to a large serving bowl and set aside.

Heat 2 tablespoons olive oil in a large skillet over high heat. Add shrimp, broccoli, garlic, and bean condiment and sauté 1 ½ minutes. Add stock, 2 tablespoons fish sauce, oyster sauce, vinegar, white pepper, and red pepper and bring to boil. Slowly add flour/water mixture, stirring constantly to prevent lumps, and return to boil. Pour mixture over cooked noodles and serve.

Red Noodles

I really don't know why I call this dish Red Noodles; it isn't red. While attending college in Blythe, California, I made it for a friend, and he enjoyed it so much that he asked what it was called. Maybe the inspiration for the name came from the paper I was writing for my U.S. history and government class—the subject was the Cold War.

¼ CUP OLIVE OIL

16 UNCOOKED MEDIUM SHRIMP (21 TO 25 PER POUND), SHELLED AND DEVEINED, OR 8 OUNCES SLICED BEEF, CHICKEN, OR PORK

12 OUNCES BROCCOLI FLORETS (ABOUT 1¾ POUNDS BEFORE TRIMMING)

1 TABLESPOON THAI OR CHINESE BEAN CONDIMENT

1 TABLESPOON FINELY CHOPPED GARLIC

2 TABLESPOONS THAI FISH SAUCE

2 TABLESPOONS THAI SWEET BLACK BEAN SAUCE

1 TABLESPOON RICE VINEGAR

1 TEASPOON WHITE PEPPER

½ TEASPOON CRUSHED RED PEPPER OR CAYENNE PEPPER

20 OUNCES FRESH RICE NOODLES, CUT INTO 1-INCH-WIDE STRIPS

3 OUNCES FRESH BEAN SPROUTS

Heat olive oil in a large skillet over high heat. Add shrimp, broccoli, bean condiment, and garlic and sauté 1½ minutes. Add all remaining ingredients except bean sprouts and cook, stirring constantly, 3 minutes. Add bean sprouts and mix in thoroughly. Remove from heat, transfer to a platter, and serve.

CHICKEN NOODLES ALFONSE

For the past decade my buddy Alfonse Ruggiero, Jr., and I have been talking about producing a movie together in Thailand—but I'll need to sell a lot more noodles before I can finance it. Like every other Tom, Dick, and Harry in Hollywood, I have a fantastic script, a great action story, a hero you can root for, an exciting ending, even a sequel. Everyone wants to make a movie in Tinseltown, so thanks for buying this book and helping to bankroll my dream.

¼ CUP OLIVE OIL

4 TEASPOONS CHOPPED GARLIC

8 OUNCES CHICKEN BREAST MEAT, CUT INTO SMALL PIECES

1½ POUNDS FRESH RICE NOODLES, CUT INTO 1-INCH-WIDE STRIPS

2 EGGS, BEATEN

2 TABLESPOONS THAI FISH SAUCE

2 TEASPOONS MAGGI SAUCE (OPTIONAL)

1 TEASPOON WHITE PEPPER

½ TEASPOON CRUSHED RED PEPPER OR CAYENNE PEPPER

¼ CUP CRUSHED UNSALTED PEANUTS

4 OUNCES FRESH BEAN SPROUTS

2 ROMAINE LETTUCE LEAVES, WASHED, DRIED, AND CUT INTO BITE-SIZE PIECES

¼ CUP THINLY SLICED LEEKS

3 TABLESPOONS DICED SCALLIONS

Heat olive oil in a large skillet over high heat. Add garlic and sauté until lightly browned, about 1 minute. Add chicken and sauté 1½ minutes. Add noodles, eggs, fish sauce, Maggi sauce, white pepper, and red pepper and cook, stirring constantly, 3 minutes. Add peanuts and bean sprouts and mix well; remove from heat. Arrange romaine on a platter and top with chicken-noodle mixture. Sprinkle with leeks and scallions and serve.

SPICY MINT NOODLES

Bryan Miller, the New York Times *restaurant critic, says that this is one of his very favorite noodle dishes; it's spicy, soothing, and refreshing at the same time. The mint, which I grow in an herb garden that my dad tends, gives a terrific earthy flavor. Start growing your own mint, because you'll want to make this delicious dish often.*

¼ CUP OLIVE OIL

1 TABLESPOON FINELY CHOPPED
   GARLIC

16 UNCOOKED MEDIUM SHRIMP (21 TO
   25 PER POUND), SHELLED AND
   DEVEINED, OR 8 OUNCES CLEANED
   SQUID, SLICED INTO RINGS

1 CUP SLICED ONIONS

⅓ CUP DICED RED BELL PEPPER

2 TEASPOONS FINELY CHOPPED
   SERRANO CHILI

¾ CUP DICED TOMATOES

2 TABLESPOONS THAI FISH SAUCE

2 TABLESPOONS THAI SWEET BLACK
   BEAN SAUCE

2 TEASPOONS MAGGI SAUCE
   (OPTIONAL)

1½ TEASPOONS RICE VINEGAR

1 TEASPOON BLACK PEPPER

26 OUNCES FRESH RICE NOODLES, CUT
   INTO 1-INCH-WIDE STRIPS

4 OUNCES FRESH BEAN SPROUTS

¼ CUP CHOPPED MINT LEAVES

4 SPRIGS MINT (GARNISH)

Heat olive oil in a large skillet over high heat. Add garlic and sauté until lightly browned, about 1 minute. Add shrimp, onions, bell pepper, and serrano chili and sauté 1 minute. Add tomatoes, fish sauce, black bean sauce, Maggi sauce, vinegar, and black pepper and sauté 1 minute. Add rice noodles and stir until heated through and well coated with sauce, about 2 minutes. Stir in bean sprouts and chopped mint. Transfer mixture to a platter, garnish with mint sprigs, and serve.

VEGETARIAN NOODLES

You mix the vegetables and throw in the noodles. What could be easier?

10 OUNCES PAD THAI (*SEN CHAN*) NOODLES

8 CUPS COLD WATER

¼ CUP OLIVE OIL

2 TEASPOONS FINELY CHOPPED GARLIC

3 OUNCES BROCCOLI FLORETS (ABOUT 1 CUP)

¾ CUP SLICED ONIONS

⅔ CUP SLICED SNOW PEAS

½ CUP DICED CELERY

¼ CUP JULIENNED CARROTS

¼ CUP DICED RED BELL PEPPER

¼ CUP DICED MUSHROOMS

3 TABLESPOONS CRUSHED UNSALTED PEANUTS

2 TABLESPOONS THAI FISH SAUCE

2 TABLESPOONS THAI SWEET BLACK BEAN SAUCE

1 TABLESPOON RICE VINEGAR

2 TEASPOONS SOY SAUCE

1 TEASPOON WHITE PEPPER

3 OUNCES FRESH BEAN SPROUTS

2 TABLESPOONS THINLY SLICED LEEKS

In a large bowl, soak noodles in cold water 45 minutes. Drain in a colander and set aside.

Heat olive oil in a large skillet over high heat. Add garlic and sauté until lightly browned, about 1 minute. Add broccoli, onions, snow peas, celery, carrots, bell pepper, and mushrooms and stir-fry 1 minute. Add peanuts, fish sauce, black bean sauce, vinegar, soy sauce, white pepper, and reserved drained noodles and cook, stirring constantly, until heated through and well mixed, about 2 minutes. Transfer to a platter, sprinkle with bean sprouts and leeks, and serve.

Seafood Pasta with Curry Cream Sauce

I like to eat at restaurants other than my own, and pasta is always one of my favorite dishes. After a while it seemed I had tried them all, so I had to start creating my own variations. This is one of them.

8 CUPS BOILING WATER

1 ½ TEASPOONS VEGETABLE OIL

¼ TEASPOON SALT

12 OUNCES FRESH LINGUINE

2 TABLESPOONS OLIVE OIL

1 TABLESPOON UNSALTED BUTTER

1 TABLESPOON FINELY CHOPPED RED ONIONS

1 TABLESPOON FINELY CHOPPED GARLIC

1 TABLESPOON FINELY CHOPPED, PEELED FRESH GINGER

1 CUP COCONUT MILK (SEE PAGE 112)

1 ½ TABLESPOONS THAI FISH SAUCE

1 TABLESPOON CURRY POWDER

1 TEASPOON WHITE PEPPER

1 CUP WHIPPING CREAM

8 MANILA OR LITTLENECK CLAMS, CLEANED

8 MEDIUM SEA SCALLOPS (10 TO 12 PER POUND)

8 MEDIUM SHRIMP (21 TO 25 PER POUND), SHELLED AND DEVEINED

4 LARGE SNOW CRAB CLAWS

4 MUSSELS, SCRUBBED AND DEBEARDED

2 TABLESPOONS FINELY DICED TOMATOES

4 SPRIGS CILANTRO (GARNISH)

Bring water to boil in a stockpot with vegetable oil and salt. Drop in pasta and boil until al dente, about 1 ½ to 2 minutes. Drain.

Meanwhile, heat olive oil and butter in a large saucepan over high heat. Add onions, garlic, and ginger and stir until garlic is lightly browned, about 2 minutes. Add coconut milk, fish sauce, curry powder, and pepper and bring to boil, stirring constantly. Add cream and return to boil, stirring. Add all seafood, reduce heat to low, and simmer 7 minutes, stirring once every minute.

Remove seafood from curry sauce and transfer to a large bowl. Add cooked pasta to sauce and toss to coat. Transfer pasta to a platter and arrange seafood over it. Top with tomatoes, garnish with cilantro, and serve.

Curry Fried Rice

The first time I tried this rice, I was at a Moslem wedding. The wonderful aroma that was steaming out of a huge clay pot was unbearable, especially since the ceremony just went on and on and my stomach was screaming for food, but the wait was surely worth it.

¼ CUP OLIVE OIL

¼ CUP THINLY SLICED SHALLOTS

1 TABLESPOON FINELY CHOPPED GARLIC

8 OUNCES CHICKEN BREAST MEAT, CUT INTO SMALL PIECES

4 CUPS COOKED WHITE RICE (SEE PAGE 113)

2 TABLESPOONS THAI FISH SAUCE

½ CUP RAW PEAS

⅓ CUP SLICED RED BELL PEPPER

1 TABLESPOON CURRY POWDER

2 TEASPOONS TOMMY TANG'S THAI SEASONING

1 TEASPOON GROUND CORIANDER

1 TEASPOON GROUND CUMIN

¼ CUP DICED SCALLIONS

4 SPRIGS CILANTRO (GARNISH)

Heat olive oil in a large skillet over high heat. Add shallots and garlic and sauté until lightly browned, about 2 minutes. Add chicken and stir-fry 1½ minutes. Add rice, fish sauce, peas, bell pepper, and seasonings and stir-fry 3 minutes. Transfer to a serving platter and sprinkle with scallions. Garnish with cilantro and serve.

PINEAPPLE FRIED RICE

As you may have heard, Thailand has two seasons—hot and damn hot. One blazing day I walked into a restaurant in Bangkok and spotted a customer with a pineapple in front of him. It gave off icy-looking vapor in the hot room, and it looked so refreshing that I told the waiter I wanted one just like it. When it arrived at the table I could hardly wait to cut that pineapple open—until I saw that the "vapor" was actually steam from the red-hot fried rice inside. I nearly fell out of my chair.

¼ CUP OLIVE OIL

2 TEASPOONS FINELY CHOPPED GARLIC

16 MEDIUM SHRIMP (21 TO 25 PER POUND), SHELLED AND DEVEINED

1 TABLESPOON ROASTED CHILI PASTE

4 CUPS COOKED WHITE RICE (SEE PAGE 113)

1 CUP DRAINED CRUSHED FRESH OR CANNED-IN-JUICE PINEAPPLE

¾ CUP SLICED RED ONIONS

⅓ CUP DICED TOMATOES

2 TABLESPOONS TOMATO PASTE

2 TABLESPOONS THAI FISH SAUCE

1 TEASPOON WHITE PEPPER

¼ CUP DICED SCALLIONS

4 SPRIGS CILANTRO (GARNISH)

Heat olive oil in a large skillet over high heat. Add garlic and sauté until lightly browned, about 1 minute. Add shrimp and chili paste and stir-fry 1½ minutes. Add rice, pineapple, onions, diced tomatoes, tomato paste, fish sauce, and white pepper and cook, stirring constantly, 4 minutes. Transfer to a platter and sprinkle with scallions. Garnish with cilantro and serve.

Spicy Mint Fried Rice

Life can be a bore sometimes, so why make the situation worse with bland rice? This cheerful combination spices things up with fresh mint, chili, and garlic. Have a nice day.

¼ CUP OLIVE OIL

1 TABLESPOON FINELY CHOPPED GARLIC

16 MEDIUM SHRIMP (21 TO 25 PER POUND) SHELLED AND DEVEINED, OR 8 OUNCES SLICED CHICKEN, BEEF, PORK, OR SQUID

2 TEASPOONS FINELY CHOPPED SERRANO CHILI

4 CUPS COOKED WHITE OR BROWN RICE (SEE PAGE 113)

⅔ CUP SLICED SNOW PEAS

½ CUP SLICED ONIONS

⅓ CUP DICED RED BELL PEPPER

⅓ CUP DICED TOMATOES

2 TABLESPOONS THAI FISH SAUCE

2 TABLESPOONS THAI SWEET BLACK BEAN SAUCE

2 TABLESPOONS CHOPPED FRESH MINT LEAVES

1 TEASPOON BLACK PEPPER

1 SPRIG MINT (GARNISH)

Heat olive oil in a large skillet over high heat. Add garlic and sauté until lightly browned, about 1 minute. Add shrimp and serrano chili and stir-fry 1 minute. Add all remaining ingredients except mint sprig and cook, stirring constantly, 3 minutes. Transfer to a platter, garnish with mint sprigs and serve.

Duck Fried Rice

A customer who dined at our New York City restaurant ordered Tommy's Duck and wasn't able to finish it. He asked a waitress to wrap it in a doggie bag. "It's for my dog," he said. While she was wrapping it, he asked her for extra honey ginger sauce. She smiled and said, "What a lucky dog." So, whenever you have leftover roast or Peking duck, save it for this dish—and if it's in a restaurant, don't forget the doggie bag.

¼ CUP OLIVE OIL

2 TEASPOONS FINELY CHOPPED GARLIC

6 OUNCES SHREDDED DUCK MEAT, RAW
  OR COOKED

¾ CUP SLICED ONIONS

⅔ CUP SLICED SNOW PEAS

½ CUP JULIENNED CARROTS

⅓ CUP DICED TOMATOES

¼ CUP DICED CELERY

¼ CUP DICED RED BELL PEPPER

1 OUNCE THINLY SLICED, PEELED
  FRESH GINGER

4 CUPS COOKED WHITE OR BROWN
  RICE (SEE PAGE 113)

2 TABLESPOONS THAI FISH SAUCE

1 TABLESPOON THAI SWEET BLACK
  BEAN SAUCE

1 TABLESPOON SOY SAUCE

1 TEASPOON BLACK PEPPER

2 TABLESPOONS DICED SCALLIONS

4 SPRIGS CILANTRO (GARNISH)

Heat olive oil in a large skillet over high heat. Add garlic and sauté until lightly browned, about 1 minute. add duck and stir-fry 1 minute. Add onions, snow peas, carrots, tomatoes, celery, bell pepper, and ginger and stir-fry 1 minute. Add rice, fish sauce, black bean sauce, soy sauce, and black pepper and cook 3 minutes, stirring constantly. Transfer to a platter and sprinkle with scallions. Garnish with cilantro and serve.

VEGETARIAN FRIED RICE

For a clue to the preparation of this dish, see the introduction to the recipe for Vegetarian Noodles on page 62.

3 TABLESPOONS OLIVE OIL

1 ½ TEASPOONS FINELY CHOPPED GARLIC

3 OUNCES SMALL BROCCOLI FLORETS (ABOUT 1 CUP)

¾ CUP SLICED ONIONS

⅔ CUP SLICED SNOW PEAS

⅔ CUP DICED TOMATOES

¼ CUP DICED MUSHROOMS

¼ CUP JULIENNED CARROTS

¼ CUP DICED CELERY

¼ CUP DICED RED BELL PEPPER

4 CUPS COOKED WHITE OR BROWN RICE (SEE PAGE 113)

2 TABLESPOONS OYSTER SAUCE

1 ½ TABLESPOONS THAI FISH SAUCE

1 TEASPOON BLACK PEPPER

2 TABLESPOONS DICED SCALLIONS

¼ CUP THINLY SLICED LEEKS

Heat olive oil in a large skillet over high heat. Add garlic and sauté until lightly browned, about 1 minute. Add broccoli, onions, snow peas, tomatoes, mushrooms, carrots, celery, and bell pepper and stir-fry 1 minute. Add rice, oyster sauce, fish sauce, and black pepper and cook, stirring constantly, 3 minutes. Transfer to a platter, sprinkle with scallions and leeks, and serve.

Black Olive Fried Rice

The Italian Trade Commissioner will love me—this dish uses not only olive oil, but black olives too. Maybe I should have made it with pasta instead of rice!

¼ CUP OLIVE OIL

1 TABLESPOON FINELY CHOPPED, PEELED FRESH GINGER

2 TEASPOONS FINELY CHOPPED GARLIC

½ CUP CHOPPED BLACK OLIVES

4 CUPS COOKED BROWN RICE (SEE PAGE 113)

2 TABLESPOONS THAI FISH SAUCE

1 TABLESPOON THAI SWEET BLACK BEAN SAUCE

2 TEASPOONS WHITE PEPPER

2 TABLESPOONS CHICKEN STOCK (SEE PAGE 110)

2 TABLESPOONS FINELY DICED RED BELL PEPPER

3 TABLESPOONS FINELY DICED SCALLIONS

2 TABLESPOONS FINELY DICED TOMATOES

1 ½ TABLESPOONS FINELY CHOPPED CILANTRO

Heat olive oil in a large skillet over high heat. Add ginger and garlic and sauté until lightly browned, about 1½ minutes. Add olives and stir-fry 1 minute. Add rice, fish sauce, black bean sauce, and white pepper and cook, stirring constantly 3 minutes. Add chicken stock and cook, stirring, 2 more minutes. Transfer to a platter. Sprinkle with bell pepper, scallions, tomatoes, and cilantro and serve.

Bangkok Jambalaya

I hope I'm not stepping on Chef Paul Prudhomme's toes in inventing this dish.

8 CUPS WATER

1 ¼ CUPS WILD RICE

1 ½ CUPS TOMATO PUREE (SEE
PAGE 111)

1 ½ CUPS RED BELL PEPPER PUREE
(SEE PAGE 111)

1 CUP LEMON GRASS STOCK OR
CHICKEN STOCK (SEE PAGE 110)

¾ CUP DICED TOMATOES

¾ CUP SLICED ONIONS

2 ½ TABLESPOONS THAI FISH SAUCE

2 TABLESPOONS FINELY CHOPPED
FRESH LEMON GRASS

1 TABLESPOON FINELY CHOPPED
GARLIC

2 TABLESPOONS TOMMY TANG'S THAI
SEASONING

2 TEASPOONS CAYENNE PEPPER

2 TEASPOONS GROUND CORIANDER

2 TEASPOONS GROUND CUMIN

4 WHOLE KAFFIR LIME LEAVES OR BAY
LEAVES

12 MANILA CLAMS OR LITTLENECK
CLAMS, SCRUBBED

8 MUSSELS, SCRUBBED AND
DEBEARDED

8 SEA SCALLOPS (10 TO 12 PER
POUND)

8 MEDIUM SHRIMP, IN SHELL (21 TO
25 PER POUND)

8 SNOW CRAB CLAWS

2 OUNCES CLEANED SQUID, CUT INTO
1-INCH RINGS

2 OUNCES HALIBUT OR TUNA, CUT INTO
1-INCH SQUARES

¼ CUP DICED SCALLIONS

Bring water to boil in a large saucepan over high heat. Add wild rice and boil 30 minutes. Reduce heat to medium-high and cook 20 more minutes. Drain wild rice in a strainer and set aside.

Combine tomato puree, pepper puree, stock, diced tomatoes, onions, fish sauce, lemon grass, garlic, and seasonings in large stockpot and bring to boil. Stir in cooked wild rice and seafood and cook 10 minutes, stirring every 2 to 3 minutes. Reduce heat to low, cover, and simmer 10 minutes longer.

Remove seafood from mixture and arrange around edge of serving bowl. Place wild rice mixture in center. Sprinkle with scallions and serve.

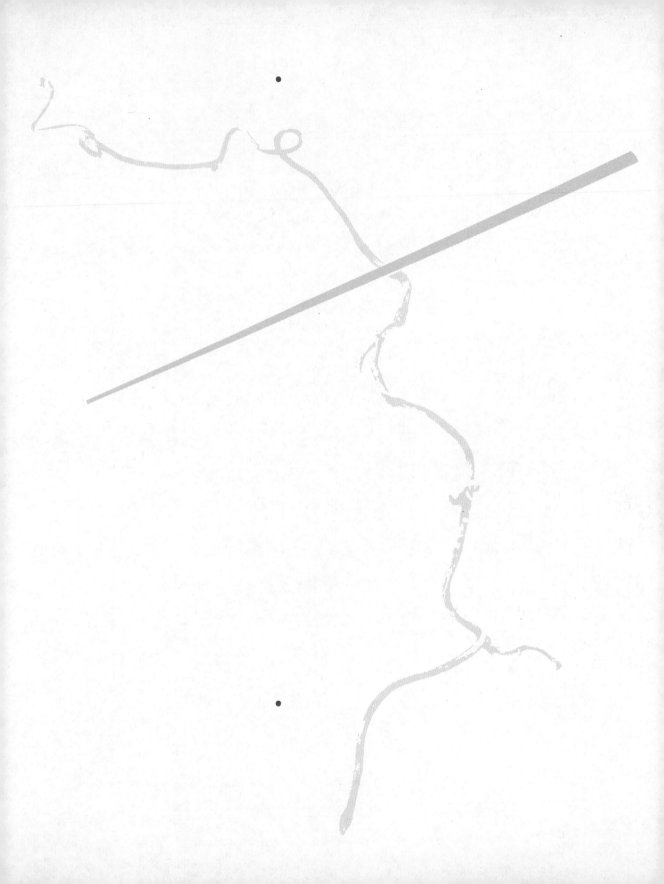

MAIN DISHES

CURRIES

There are many varieties of Thai curry paste, with different textures, flavors, and preparation methods. Some types are overpoweringly spicy for the Western palate, but the four most popular—Panang, red, green, and mussamun—have universal appeal. They're also my personal favorites.

SHRIMP PANANG

There's a myth about Asian (and particularly Thai) food that says it's hard, or at least complicated, to prepare. Baloney! Take this dish—it's absolutely simple to make and it tastes out of this world. All you need are a few commonsense guidelines. In a very short time you'll be an expert.

20 LARGE SHRIMP (13 TO 15 PER POUND), SHELLED AND DEVEINED, TAIL LEFT INTACT
¼ CUP OLIVE OIL
1 ½ TABLESPOONS TOMMY TANG'S THAI SEASONING

2 TABLESPOONS OLIVE OIL
2 TABLESPOONS FINELY CHOPPED RED ONIONS
4 TEASPOONS FINELY CHOPPED GARLIC
½ CUP COCONUT MILK (SEE PAGE 112)

1 TABLESPOON PANANG CURRY PASTE
1 TABLESPOON THAI FISH SAUCE
2 TEASPOONS PAPRIKA
½ CUP WHIPPING CREAM

2 CUPS WATER
16 SNOW PEAS

12 THIN SLICES RED BELL PEPPER (GARNISH)

Combine shrimp, ¼ cup olive oil, and Thai seasoning in a large bowl and mix until shrimp are well coated. Cover bowl with plastic wrap and refrigerate at least 1 hour.

Prepare charcoal grill if using. Grill or cook the shrimp in a large skillet over high heat just until opaque, 2½ to 3 minutes on each side over charcoal or 2 minutes on each side in skillet. Arrange on 1 side of each of 4 plates.

Heat 2 tablespoons olive oil in a medium skillet over high heat. Add onions and garlic and sauté until lightly browned, about 1½ minutes. Add coconut milk, curry paste, fish sauce, and paprika, reduce heat to medium, and cook, stirring constantly, for 2 minutes. Add cream and bring to boil, then reduce heat to low and simmer until sauce is reduced by half, about 3 to 4 minutes.

Meanwhile, bring water to boil in a large saucepan. Drop in snow peas and boil 1 minute. Drain and pat dry. Spread sauce over center of each serving plate. Arrange snow peas on opposite side of plate from shrimp. Garnish with bell pepper and serve.

Red Curry Shrimp

Most Thai chefs make their curries very watery—more like what Westerners would think of as a curry broth. They also have a tendency to overcook the coconut milk, so that it breaks down and the oil separates out; this, of course, makes the mixture very greasy. I prefer a thick, creamy curry and I don't let the coconut milk turn to oil. You'll see; this sauce tastes like a curry should.

¼ CUP OLIVE OIL

1 TABLESPOON FINELY CHOPPED
 RED ONIONS

1 ½ TEASPOONS FINELY CHOPPED
 GARLIC

1 ½ CUPS COCONUT MILK
 (SEE PAGE 112)

1 TABLESPOON THAI RED CURRY PASTE

4 KAFFIR LIME LEAVES OR SUBSTITUTE
 LEMON LEAVES

2 TABLESPOONS CHOPPED THAI OR
 REGULAR BASIL

1 ½ TABLESPOONS THAI FISH SAUCE

1 CUP YELLOW SQUASH OR ZUCCHINI
 CUT INTO ¼-INCH-THICK SLICES

1 CUP WHIPPING CREAM

½ CUP JULIENNED RED BELL PEPPER

1 TEASPOON ALL-PURPOSE FLOUR
 MIXED WITH 1 TABLESPOON COLD
 WATER

1 ½ POUNDS LARGE SHRIMP (13 TO
 15 PER POUND), SHELLED AND
 DEVEINED

4 SPRIGS BASIL (GARNISH)

Heat olive oil in a large saucepan over high heat. Add onions and garlic and sauté until lightly browned, about 1 minute. Add coconut milk and curry paste and cook, stirring constantly, 3 minutes. Add lime leaves, basil, and fish sauce and bring to boil. Add squash, cream, bell pepper, and flour/water mixture and return to boil. Reduce heat to low and simmer until sauce is thick, about 15 minutes. Add shrimp and bring to boil; let boil 2 minutes. Transfer curry to a bowl, garnish with basil, and serve.

Alaska King Crab Curry

I should eliminate this dish from my menu; the crab is so expensive, even wholesale, that I don't make a dime on it. But my attorney, Carl Grumer, who is also a close family friend, loves it—so, Carl, here's the recipe. Now you can make it at home so I don't have to lose money. By the way, use a heavy cleaver to cut the crab legs into 4-inch lengths, shell and all; this makes them easier to eat and helps them cook evenly.

3 TABLESPOONS OLIVE OIL

1 ½ TABLESPOONS FINELY CHOPPED
    RED ONIONS

1 ½ TEASPOONS FINELY CHOPPED
    GARLIC

1 ½ TEASPOONS FINELY CHOPPED,
    PEELED FRESH GINGER

4 POUNDS ALASKA KING CRAB LEGS,
    CUT INTO 4-INCH LENGTHS

¾ CUP COCONUT MILK (SEE PAGE 112)

1 ½ TABLESPOONS CURRY POWDER

¾ CUP WHIPPING CREAM

½ CUP RED BELL PEPPER CUT INTO
    ½-INCH SQUARES

½ CUP ONIONS CUT INTO ½-INCH
    CUBES

½ CUP CELERY CUT INTO ½-INCH
    CUBES

½ CUP SLICED SNOW PEAS

1 TABLESPOON THAI FISH SAUCE

1 TEASPOON BLACK PEPPER

1 TEASPOON ALL-PURPOSE FLOUR
    MIXED WITH 1 TABLESPOON COLD
    WATER

Heat olive oil in a large saucepan over high heat. Add onions, garlic, and ginger and sauté until lightly browned, about 1½ minutes. Add crab, coconut milk, and curry powder and cook, stirring constantly, 2 minutes. Add all remaining ingredients and bring to boil, stirring. Reduce heat to low and simmer 5 minutes. Transfer to a platter and serve.

Green Curry Salmon

Green is a color always associated with fresh, light, spring-season foods. Here, the green sauce and pink salmon make a beautiful combination. Kra-chai is a root with the elusive flavor of ginger, turmeric, and galanga. It's admittedly hard to find, so if you can't, just leave it out.

¼ CUP OLIVE OIL

1 TABLESPOON FINELY CHOPPED RED ONIONS

1 ½ TEASPOONS FINELY CHOPPED GARLIC

1 ½ CUPS COCONUT MILK (SEE PAGE 112)

2 TABLESPOONS GREEN CURRY PASTE

1 CUP EGGPLANT CUT INTO ¾-INCH CUBES

1 CUP WHIPPING CREAM

½ CUP SLICED BAMBOO SHOOTS

½ CUP ANAHEIM CHILI OR GREEN BELL PEPPER PUREE (SEE PAGE 111)

8 KAFFIR LIME LEAVES OR SUBSTITUTE LEMON LEAVES

1 ½ TABLESPOONS THAI FISH SAUCE

2 TABLESPOONS CHOPPED THAI OR REGULAR BASIL

1 ½ TEASPOONS SUGAR OR HONEY

1 TEASPOON FINELY CHOPPED *KRA-CHAI* (OPTIONAL)

1 TEASPOON ALL-PURPOSE FLOUR MIXED WITH 1 TABLESPOON COLD WATER

1 POUND SALMON STEAKS, CUT INTO 1-INCH CUBES

4 SPRIGS BASIL (GARNISH)

Heat olive oil in a large saucepan over high heat. Add onions and garlic and sauté until lightly browned, about 1½ minutes. Add coconut milk and curry paste and cook, stirring to remove lumps, for 3 minutes. Add eggplant, whipping cream, bamboo shoots, pepper puree, lime leaves, fish sauce, basil, sugar, *kra-chai*, and flour/water mixture and return to boil. Reduce heat to low and simmer until thick, about 15 minutes, stirring every 5 minutes. Add salmon, increase heat to high, and boil 2 minutes. Transfer curry to a bowl, garnish with basil, and serve.

CHICKEN CURRY

I've had this on the menu ever since I started cooking professionally. Every so often I OD on Chicken Curry and try to stop serving it for a while, but everyone insists that it stay.

¼ CUP OLIVE OIL

1 TABLESPOON FINELY CHOPPED
   RED ONIONS

1 ½ TEASPOONS FINELY CHOPPED
   GARLIC

1 ½ CUPS COCONUT MILK
   (SEE PAGE 112)

1 TABLESPOON THAI RED CURRY PASTE

1 ½ TABLESPOONS CURRY POWDER

1 ½ TABLESPOONS THAI FISH SAUCE

1 ¼ POUNDS CHICKEN BREAST MEAT,
   CUT INTO ¾-INCH CUBES

1 CUP CARROTS CUT INTO 1-INCH
   LENGTHS

1 CUP BOILING POTATO CUT INTO
   1-INCH CUBES

1 CUP WHIPPING CREAM

1 TEASPOON ALL-PURPOSE FLOUR
   MIXED WITH 1 TABLESPOON COLD
   WATER

Heat olive oil in a large saucepan over high heat. Add onions and garlic and stir until lightly browned, about 1½ minutes. Add coconut milk and curry paste and cook, stirring, 3 minutes. Add curry powder and fish sauce and bring to boil. Add all remaining ingredients and return to boil. Reduce heat to low and simmer until sauce is thick and creamy, about 15 minutes. Transfer to a bowl and serve.

PANANG CHICKEN

I'll forgive you if you make this with shrimp, beef, pork, lobster, or anything you like instead of chicken. You can't imagine how many dishes you can create with Panang curry paste—as Billy Crystal would say, it's maaahvelous.

3 TABLESPOONS OLIVE OIL

2 TABLESPOONS FINELY CHOPPED
   RED ONIONS

1 TABLESPOON FINELY CHOPPED
   GARLIC

1 TABLESPOON PANANG CURRY PASTE

1 POUND SLICED CHICKEN BREAST
   MEAT

½ CUP COCONUT MILK (SEE PAGE 112)

1 TABLESPOON THAI FISH SAUCE

1 TABLESPOON PAPRIKA

1 CUP SLICED SNOW PEAS

½ CUP DICED RED BELL PEPPER

½ CUP WHIPPING CREAM

Heat olive oil in a large skillet over high heat. Add onions, garlic, and curry paste and cook 1 minute, stirring constantly. Add chicken, coconut milk, fish sauce, and paprika and cook, stirring constantly, until reduced by half, about 3 minutes. Add snow peas, bell pepper, and whipping cream and cook until sauce is creamy and slightly thickened, about 2 minutes. Transfer to a platter and serve.

Lamb Mussamun

Lamb Mussamun is an Indian curry of Moslem origin. Thai chefs like to use beef instead of lamb, but I'm different from most Thai.

¼ CUP OLIVE OIL

2 TABLESPOONS FINELY CHOPPED RED ONIONS

1 TABLESPOON FINELY CHOPPED GARLIC

2 CUPS COCONUT MILK (SEE PAGE 112)

2 TABLESPOONS MUSSAMUN CURRY PASTE

1½ POUNDS LAMB TENDERLOIN, CUT INTO 1-INCH CUBES

2 MEDIUM POTATOES, PEELED AND CUT INTO 1-INCH CUBES

8 WHOLE SHALLOTS, PEELED

½ CUP ROASTED UNSALTED CASHEWS

½ CUP TAMARIND JUICE (SEE PAGE 112)

2 TABLESPOONS THAI FISH SAUCE

2 STICKS CINNAMON

16 CARDAMOM SEEDS

1½ TEASPOONS SUGAR

1½ CUPS WHIPPING CREAM

1½ TEASPOONS ALL-PURPOSE FLOUR MIXED WITH 2 TABLESPOONS COLD WATER

Heat olive oil in a large saucepan over high heat. Add onions and garlic and stir until lightly browned, about 1½ minutes. Add coconut milk and curry paste and cook, stirring constantly, 2 minutes. Add lamb, potatoes, shallots, cashews, tamarind juice, fish sauce, spices, and sugar and cook, stirring every 2 minutes, until sauce is reduced by half, about 8 to 10 minutes. Add cream and flour/water mixture, reduce heat to low, and simmer 20 minutes. Transfer to bowl and serve.

The Original Tommy's Duck with Honey Ginger Sauce

Some people will say that naming a dish after yourself is egomaniacal. But I don't think there's anything wrong in promoting something that's yours, and that you believe in. Look at Donald Trump—a great self-promoter with a lot of guts and a last name that starts with T. Let me think of what else we have in common . . . okay, I know. If he stops making money now and waits a couple of thousand years I may catch up with him.

1 CUP WATER

½ CUP LIGHT SOY SAUCE

½ CUP GROUND ONIONS (GRIND IN A
   FOOD PROCESSOR)

¼ CUP GROUND, PEELED FRESH GINGER
   (GRIND IN A FOOD PROCESSOR)

2 LONG ISLAND DUCKLINGS (5½ TO
   6 POUNDS TOTAL), SPLIT IN HALF

3 CUPS VEGETABLE OIL (FOR DEEP
   FRYING)

HONEY GINGER SAUCE

1 CUP HONEY

½ CUP WATER

¼ CUP PLUM SAUCE

¼ CUP SOY SAUCE

4 OUNCES FRESH GINGER, SLICED

1 TEASPOON ALL-PURPOSE FLOUR
   MIXED WITH 2 TABLESPOONS COLD
   WATER

Combine first 4 ingredients and coat ducks thoroughly with mixture. Cover ducks and refrigerate at least 6 hours, preferably overnight. Remove ducks from marinade, wiping off excess, reserve marinade.

Preheat oven to 350° F. Place ducks in a roasting pan and strain 1 cup marinade over them. Roast 1½ hours, basting every 15 minutes with juices in pan.

Heat oil in a large saucepan or a deep frying pan to 350° F. Place 1 duck half skin-side-down in oil and deep-fry until skin is crisp, 3 to 5 minutes. Remove with tongs and drain on paper towels. Repeat with remaining duck, frying halves 1 piece at a time. If desired, bone duck, or cut into serving pieces or slices before serving.

For ginger sauce, combine honey, water, plum sauce, soy sauce, and ginger in a small saucepan and bring to boil over high heat. Stir in flour/water mixture, reduce heat to low, and simmer until sauce is syrupy, about 20 minutes. Serve ducks hot or at room temperature; pour sauce over ducks or pass separately.

SPICY MINT CHICKEN

I love mint; its flavor is so refreshing and soothing. All it needs is water, decent soil, and not even much sun, so try growing your own. Since our garden is full of mint, I'm always trying to invent more recipes that use it.

6 TABLESPOONS OLIVE OIL
2 TABLESPOONS FINELY CHOPPED RED ONIONS
2 TABLESPOONS FINELY CHOPPED GARLIC
1 ¼ POUNDS SLICED CHICKEN BREAST MEAT
1 ½ TEASPOONS FINELY CHOPPED SERRANO CHILI
1 CUP SLICED ONIONS
½ CUP DICED RED BELL PEPPER

½ CUP DICED TOMATOES
1 TABLESPOON THAI FISH SAUCE
1 TABLESPOON THAI SWEET BLACK BEAN SAUCE
1 ½ TEASPOONS MAGGI SAUCE (OPTIONAL)
½ CUP LEMON GRASS STOCK OR CHICKEN STOCK (SEE PAGE 110)
3 TABLESPOONS CHOPPED MINT LEAVES
SPRIGS MINT (GARNISH)

Heat olive oil in a medium skillet over high heat. Add red onions and garlic and sauté until lightly browned, about 1 ½ minutes. Add chicken and serrano chili and stir-fry 2 minutes. Add all remaining ingredients except mint sprigs and cook, stirring constantly, 3 minutes. Transfer to a platter, garnish with mint, and serve.

Spicy BBQ Chicken with Sweet Chili Sauce

People ask for this recipe a lot, but knowing that I'd be writing a cookbook someday, I always avoided giving it out. I really should save it for my children's children. But now, for all my friends and loyal customers, here it is. All I ask in return is that when folks ask you to share the recipe you say, "Why should I? Buy a copy of Tommy's book."

MARINADE

1 ½ CUPS COCONUT MILK (SEE PAGE 112)

½ CUP CHOPPED GARLIC

¼ CUP CHOPPED FRESH GINGER

¼ CUP OLIVE OIL

2 TABLESPOONS THAI FISH SAUCE

2 TABLESPOONS CURRY POWDER

1 TABLESPOON BLACK PEPPER

1 TABLESPOON WHITE PEPPER

1 TABLESPOON SUGAR OR HONEY

1 TEASPOON TURMERIC

2 CHICKENS (ABOUT 3 POUNDS EACH), WITH BONES AND SKIN, HALVED

SWEET CHILI SAUCE

½ CUP WATER

½ CUP RICE VINEGAR

¼ CUP SUGAR

2 TABLESPOONS PLUM SAUCE

1 TABLESPOON THAI FISH SAUCE

1 TABLESPOON FRESH LIME JUICE OR LEMON JUICE

2 TEASPOONS TOMATO PASTE

1 TEASPOON FINELY CHOPPED GARLIC

½ TEASPOON FINELY CHOPPED SERRANO CHILI

½ TEASPOON GROUND RED CHILI PASTE

½ TEASPOON PAPRIKA

½ TEASPOON SALT

½ TEASPOON ALL-PURPOSE FLOUR MIXED WITH 1 TABLESPOON COLD WATER

4 SLICES FRESH PINEAPPLE

Combine all marinade ingredients in a large mixing bowl. Gently prick chicken skin all over with fork. Add chicken to marinade mixture and rub it in. Cover bowl with plastic wrap and refrigerate overnight.

Preheat oven to 350° F. Place chicken on baking tray and bake chicken until cooked through, about 45 minutes, basting with marinade every 15 minutes. (Alternatively, prepare charcoal grill. First bake chicken in preheated oven 25 minutes, then grill 10 minutes on each side to finish cooking.)

Combine all ingredients for the sauce in a small saucepan and bring to boil over high heat. Reduce heat to low and simmer 4 minutes. Let cool.

Transfer each cooked chicken half to a platter and serve with sweet chili sauce and a pineapple slice.

Lemon Grass Chicken

Don't tell me you don't know what lemon grass is. I've been serving it to you for a dozen years. Lemon grass is as Thai as hot dogs and apple pie are American. This herb is the jewel in the crown of Thai cooking; get to know it.

MARINADE

¼ CUP VIRGIN OLIVE OIL

2 TABLESPOONS TOMMY TANG'S THAI SEASONING

1 STALK LEMON GRASS (THICKER BASE OF STALK ONLY), FINELY CHOPPED (RESERVE LEAVES)

4 BONED HALF CHICKEN BREASTS (7 TO 8 OUNCES EACH), WITH SKIN

TOPPING

½ CUP VIRGIN OLIVE OIL

2 STALKS LEMON GRASS (THICKER BASE OF STALK ONLY, 3 OUTER LAYERS REMOVED),* FINELY DICED

1 TABLESPOON CHOPPED GARLIC

¼ CUP CHOPPED UNSALTED PEANUTS

SAUCE

1½ TABLESPOONS OLIVE OIL

2 TABLESPOONS UNSALTED BUTTER

1 STALK LEMON GRASS (THICKER BASE OF STALK ONLY), FINELY CHOPPED (RESERVE LEAVES)

2 TABLESPOONS CHOPPED SHALLOTS

1 TABLESPOON CHOPPED GARLIC

2 TEASPOONS THAI FISH SAUCE

2 TEASPOONS ROASTED CHILI PASTE

¾ CUP COCONUT MILK (SEE PAGE 112)

2 TABLESPOONS GROUND UNSALTED PEANUTS

½ CUP WHIPPING CREAM

* YOU CAN USE THE OUTER STALKS OF LEMON GRASS TO MAKE LEMON GRASS STOCK (PAGE 110).

For marinade, combine ingredients in a large mixing bowl. Add chicken and rub gently with oil mixture. Cover bowl with plastic wrap and refrigerate at least 3 hours preferably overnight.

Prepare charcoal grill. Grill chicken breasts until skin is crisp, about 5 to 7 minutes on each side. (Alternatively, preheat oven to 350° F. Arrange chicken breasts on rimmed, ungreased baking sheet skin-side-up and bake 5 minutes. Turn oven to broil; broil chicken until skin is crisp, about 2 to 4 minutes.) Remove and set aside.

For topping, heat olive oil in a small saucepan over medium heat. Add lemon grass and sauté until lightly browned, 2 to 3 minutes. Remove with a slotted spoon and drain on paper towels. Add garlic to oil and sauté until lightly browned, 1 to 1½ minutes, drain on paper towels. Let lemon grass and garlic cool briefly. Mix with chopped peanuts and set aside.

For sauce, heat olive oil with butter in a medium saucepan over medium heat. Add lemon grass and sauté until lightly browned, 1–2 minutes. Add shallots and garlic and sauté 1 minute. Add fish sauce and chili paste and sauté 1 minute. Add coconut milk and ground peanuts and cook, stirring constantly, 3 minutes. Stir in cream and bring to boil. Reduce heat to low and simmer until sauce is reduced by half, about 4 to 5 minutes. Strain sauce through a fine sieve and keep warm.

Place 1 chicken breast at side of each serving plate. Pour sauce onto other side of the plate. Sprinkle chicken with topping mixture and garnish with reserved lemon grass leaves.

Dried Chili Chicken

Simple to prepare when you're pressed for time but don't want to settle for the ordinary. I find something energizing about this dish—but then I like it when my ears start smoking.

6 TABLESPOONS OLIVE OIL

1 TABLESPOON FINELY CHOPPED GARLIC

1 ¼ POUNDS SLICED CHICKEN BREAST MEAT

1 CUP ROASTED UNSALTED CASHEWS

12 SMALL DRIED WHOLE CHILIES

1 ½ TABLESPOONS ROASTED CHILI PASTE

½ CUP DICED ONIONS

½ CUP DICED RED BELL PEPPER

½ CUP SCALLIONS CUT INTO 1-INCH LENGTHS

½ CUP LEMON GRASS STOCK OR CHICKEN STOCK (SEE PAGE 110)

1 TABLESPOON THAI FISH SAUCE

1 TABLESPOON THAI SWEET BLACK BEAN SAUCE

2 TEASPOONS BLACK PEPPER

Heat olive oil in a large skillet over high heat. Add garlic and sauté until lightly browned, about 1 minute. Add chicken and stir-fry 2 minutes. Add cashews, dried chilies, and chili paste and cook, stirring constantly, 1 minute. Add all remaining ingredients and cook, stirring constantly, 3 minutes. Transfer to a platter and serve.

Siamese Chicken with Basil

Basil was my first culinary love, and it's been a long-lasting relationship. Depend on this simple dish to create a relaxed mood under candlelight.

1/4 CUP OLIVE OIL

2 TABLESPOONS TOMMY TANG'S THAI SEASONING

4 HALF CHICKEN BREASTS (7 TO 8 OUNCES EACH), BONED AND SKINNED

28 THAI OR SMALL REGULAR BASIL LEAVES

6 TABLESPOONS OLIVE OIL

5 TABLESPOONS FINELY CHOPPED RED ONIONS

2 TABLESPOONS FINELY CHOPPED GARLIC

2 TEASPOONS FINELY CHOPPED SERRANO CHILI

2 TABLESPOONS THAI SWEET BLACK BEAN SAUCE

1 TABLESPOON THAI FISH SAUCE

2 TEASPOONS MAGGI SAUCE (OPTIONAL)

1/2 CUP LEMON GRASS STOCK OR CHICKEN STOCK (SEE PAGE 110)

1/3 CUP TOMATO PUREE (SEE PAGE 111)

2 TABLESPOONS FINELY CHOPPED THAI OR REGULAR BASIL

2 TABLESPOONS FINELY DICED RED BELL PEPPER

2 TEASPOONS BLACK PEPPER

4 ROASTED ANAHEIM CHILIES* (GARNISH)

* TO ROAST CHILIES, FOLLOW INSTRUCTIONS FOR ROASTING BELL PEPPERS IN RECIPE FOR RED OR GREEN BELL PEPPER PUREE, PAGE 111

Combine 1/4 cup olive oil and Thai seasoning in a medium bowl. Add chicken and rub gently with mixture. Cover bowl with plastic wrap and refrigerate 3 hours.

Preheat charcoal grill. Grill chicken just until cooked through, about 5 to 7 minutes on each side. (Alternatively, cook in a large skillet over high heat for 3 to 4 minutes on each side.) Transfer chicken to cutting board and cut each piece into 8 slices. Insert basil leaves between slices, reassemble each breast, and place at 1 side of each serving plate. Keep warm.

Heat 6 tablespoons olive oil in a medium skillet over high heat. Add onions, garlic, and serrano chili and sauté until garlic is lightly browned, about 2 minutes. Add bean sauce, fish sauce, and Maggi sauce and cook, stirring, 1 minute. Add stock, tomato puree, chopped basil, bell pepper, and black pepper and cook, stirring constantly, 3 minutes.

Spoon 1/4 of the sauce onto each plate opposite chicken. Add a roasted chili to center of each plate and serve.

S E A F O O D

Thai Chili Fish

There's no point serving a beautiful piece of fish without a good sauce—it's like a wedding without a bride.

4 8-OUNCE TILEFISH, SEA BASS, STRIPED BASS, RED SNAPPER, OR TUNA FILLETS

2 TABLESPOONS OLIVE OIL

2 TABLESPOONS TOMMY TANG'S THAI SEASONING

3 TABLESPOONS OLIVE OIL

6 TABLESPOONS FINELY CHOPPED RED ONIONS

2 TABLESPOONS FINELY CHOPPED GARLIC

1 TABLESPOON FINELY CHOPPED OR GROUND, PEELED FRESH GINGER

2 TEASPOONS CHOPPED SERRANO CHILI

12 SHIITAKE MUSHROOMS

1 TABLESPOON ROASTED CHILI PASTE

1 TABLESPOON OYSTER SAUCE

1 TABLESPOON THAI SWEET BLACK BEAN SAUCE

2 TEASPOONS THAI FISH SAUCE

1 TEASPOON BLACK PEPPER

⅓ CUP LEMON GRASS STOCK (SEE PAGE 110)

2 TABLESPOONS FINELY DICED RED BELL PEPPER

4 SPRIGS MINT (GARNISH)

Place fish in a large mixing bowl. Coat with 2 tablespoons olive oil and Thai seasoning. Heat a large skillet over high heat and sauté fish 2 minutes on each side. Transfer to serving plates and keep warm.

Heat 3 tablespoons olive oil in a medium skillet over high heat. Add onions and garlic and sauté until lightly browned, about 1½ minutes. Add ginger and serrano chili and sauté 1 minute. Add mushrooms, chili paste, oyster sauce, black bean sauce, fish sauce, and black pepper and cook, stirring, 1 minute. Add lemon grass stock and bell pepper and cook, stirring, 2 minutes. Pour sauce evenly over fish; arrange mushrooms at side of each plate. Garnish with mint and serve.

Grilled Salmon with Kaffir Lime Sauce

Like lemon grass, kaffir limes are one of those distinctive ingredients that are essential to Thai cooking. Their flavor is like lemons but they have a stronger aroma and a unique taste.

2 TABLESPOONS OLIVE OIL

1 TABLESPOON TOMMY TANG'S THAI
 SEASONING

4 8-OUNCE SALMON FILLETS, ¾ TO
 1 INCH THICK

KAFFIR LIME SAUCE

2 TABLESPOONS UNSALTED BUTTER

2 TABLESPOONS OLIVE OIL

2 TABLESPOONS FINELY CHOPPED RED
 ONIONS

2 TABLESPOONS FINELY CHOPPED
 GARLIC

¾ CUP COCONUT MILK (SEE PAGE 112)

2 TABLESPOONS FINELY CHOPPED
 KAFFIR LIME LEAVES

1 CUP WHIPPING CREAM

2 TEASPOONS THAI FISH SAUCE

1 TEASPOON WHITE PEPPER

2 TABLESPOONS SALMON CAVIAR

4 KAFFIR LIME LEAVES (GARNISH)

Combine 2 tablespoons olive oil with Thai seasoning in a medium mixing bowl and whisk to blend well. Add salmon and toss gently until completely coated. Cover bowl with plastic wrap and refrigerate 3 hours.

Prepare charcoal grill. Grill salmon fillets 5 minutes on each side. Set aside and keep warm. Alternatively, heat 1 tablespoon olive oil in a large skillet over high heat. Add salmon fillets and sear 3 to 4 minutes on each side. Or, preheat oven broiler, place salmon fillets, coated with leftover marinade, on a thick pan and cook 5 to 6 minutes.

For sauce, melt butter with olive oil in a medium saucepan over high heat. Add onions, and garlic and sauté until lightly browned, about 2 minutes. Add coconut milk and lime leaves and bring to boil, stirring constantly. Add cream, fish sauce, and white pepper and return to boil, stirring constantly. Reduce heat to low and simmer 4 minutes. Strain sauce through a fine sieve.

Divide sauce among 4 serving plates, smoothing over entire bottom of plate. Place 1 salmon fillet on center of each plate. Sprinkle caviar over sauce, garnish with lime leaves, and serve.

GRILLED RED SNAPPER WITH ROSEMARY HONEY GLAZE

Food plays an important part in Southeast Asian New Year celebrations. Fish is considered a symbol of prosperity, and a bright red fish, served whole, is an especially popular holiday dish.

4 WHOLE RED SNAPPER (1 ¼ TO 1 ½ POUNDS EACH), SCALED AND GUTTED
4 LARGE CLOVES GARLIC, THINLY SLICED
4 SMALL SPRIGS FRESH ROSEMARY
½ CUP OLIVE OIL
¼ CUP TOMMY TANG'S THAI SEASONING

1 CUP VIRGIN OLIVE OIL
2 TABLESPOONS CHOPPED GARLIC
1 TEASPOON CHOPPED SERRANO CHILI

1 TEASPOON WHITE PEPPER
½ CUP HONEY
¼ CUP FRESH LEMON JUICE
2 TABLESPOONS RICE VINEGAR
2 TABLESPOONS FINELY CHOPPED ROSEMARY, FRESH OR DRIED
4 TEASPOONS THAI FISH SAUCE

4 6-INCH SPRIGS ROSEMARY (GARNISH)
16 2- TO 3-INCH SLICES RED BELL PEPPER (GARNISH)

Prepare barbecue grill or preheat oven to 400° F. Using poultry shears, trim fins from fish. Rinse fish with cold water and pat dry. Place garlic and rosemary sprigs inside each fish, dividing evenly. Coat fish with olive oil and Thai seasoning. Grill just until cooked through, about 7 to 9 minutes on each side, or bake 15 minutes. To test for doneness, carefully cut into the center of the fish with a small, thin knife. It should be cooked through but still very moist inside. Take care not to tear the fish when testing.

Meanwhile, heat virgin olive oil in a medium skillet over medium heat. Add garlic and stir until lightly browned. Add serrano chili and white pepper and stir 1 minute. Add honey, lemon juice, vinegar, rosemary, and fish sauce and bring to boil, stirring constantly. Cook until sauce is thickened to glaze consistency, about 3 minutes.

Arrange fish on a platter and pour rosemary honey glaze over it. Garnish with rosemary sprigs and bell pepper slices and serve.

Grilled Tuna with Roasted Red Bell Pepper Sauce

I don't like tuna without a sauce—but then it's essential to Thai cuisine that every dish be accompanied by its own sauce. This is just one of the things that make Thai cooking so exciting.

2 TABLESPOONS OLIVE OIL

1 TABLESPOON TOMMY TANG'S THAI SEASONING

4 8-OUNCE TUNA FILLETS, ¾ TO 1 INCH THICK

ROASTED RED BELL PEPPER SAUCE

2 TABLESPOONS OLIVE OIL

1 TABLESPOON FINELY CHOPPED GARLIC

1 CUP RED BELL PEPPER PUREE (SEE PAGE 111)

¼ CUP TOMATO PUREE (SEE PAGE 111)

1 TABLESPOON THAI FISH SAUCE

1½ TEASPOONS WHITE PEPPER

¼ CUP WHIPPING CREAM

4 SPRIGS BASIL (GARNISH)

Combine 2 tablespoons olive oil with Thai seasoning in a medium mixing bowl and whisk to blend well. Add tuna and toss gently until completely coated. Cover bowl with plastic wrap and refrigerate 3 hours.

Prepare charcoal grill. Grill tuna fillets 5 minutes on each side. Set aside and keep warm. If a charcoal grill is not available, preheat oven broiler, place tuna fillets, coated with the leftover marinade, on a thick pan and cook 5 to 6 minutes. To test for doneness, carefully cut into the middle of the fish with a small, thin knife. It should be cooked through but still very moist.

For sauce, heat olive oil in a medium skillet over high heat. Add garlic and sauté 1 minute. Add pepper and tomato purees, fish sauce, and white pepper and cook, stirring constantly, 3 minutes. Add cream and bring to boil. Reduce heat to low and simmer 4 minutes.

Divide sauce among 4 serving plates, smoothing over entire bottom of plate. Place 1 tuna fillet in center of each plate, garnish with basil, and serve.

SPICY MINT CALAMARI

Calamari—sounds wonderful. Let's order some! Squid—sounds awful. I don't like it. I used to call this dish "spicy mint squid" and customers stayed away from it. Now that I've borrowed the name from Italian restaurants, I can't cook it fast enough.

¼ CUP OLIVE OIL

2 TABLESPOONS FINELY CHOPPED RED
   ONIONS

1 TABLESPOON FINELY CHOPPED
   GARLIC

1 POUND CLEANED SQUID, CUT INTO
   1-INCH ROUNDS

¾ CUP SLICED ONIONS

½ CUP DICED RED BELL PEPPER

½ CUP DICED TOMATOES

¼ CUP TOMATO PUREE (SEE PAGE 111)

¼ CUP LEMON GRASS STOCK OR
   CHICKEN STOCK (SEE PAGE 110)

1 TABLESPOON OYSTER SAUCE

1 TABLESPOON THAI FISH SAUCE

1 TABLESPOON THAI SWEET BLACK
   BEAN SAUCE

1 TEASPOON FINELY CHOPPED
   SERRANO CHILI

½ TEASPOON BLACK PEPPER

3 TABLESPOONS DICED SCALLIONS

3 TABLESPOONS CHOPPED MINT LEAVES

4 SPRIGS MINT (GARNISH)

Heat olive oil in a large skillet over high heat. Add red onions and garlic, and sauté until lightly browned, about 1½ minutes. Add squid and sauté 2 minutes. Add sliced onions, bell pepper, tomatoes, tomato puree, stock, oyster sauce, fish sauce, black bean sauce, serrano chili, and black pepper and cook, stirring 2 minutes. Add scallions, and chopped mint and stir 30 seconds. Transfer to a platter, garnish with mint, and serve.

Soft-Shell Crabs with Garlic Ginger Sauce

This is my favorite crab recipe. In most restaurants, all you get along with the crabs is a lemon wedge—but wait until you try them cooked this way.

2 CUPS ALL-PURPOSE FLOUR

2 TABLESPOONS CORNSTARCH

1 TABLESPOON TOMMY TANG'S THAI SEASONING

8 LARGE SOFT-SHELL CRABS

4 CUPS VEGETABLE OIL (FOR DEEP FRYING)

GARLIC GINGER SAUCE

3 TABLESPOONS OLIVE OIL

3 TABLESPOONS FINELY CHOPPED RED ONIONS

3 TABLESPOONS FINELY CHOPPED GARLIC

2 TABLESPOONS FINELY CHOPPED, PEELED FRESH GINGER

⅓ CUP LEMON GRASS STOCK OR CHICKEN STOCK (SEE PAGE 110)

2 TABLESPOONS SOY SAUCE

2 TABLESPOONS FRESH LEMON JUICE

2 TABLESPOONS FINELY DICED RED BELL PEPPER

1 TABLESPOON THAI SWEET BLACK BEAN SAUCE

2 TEASPOONS TOMMY TANG'S THAI SEASONING

4 SPRIGS MINT (GARNISH)

Combine flour, cornstarch, and 1 tablespoon Thai seasoning in a large bowl and mix well. Add crabs at one time and coat completely. Arrange crabs on an ungreased baking sheet and let stand 1 hour; reserve flour mixture.

Using a toothpick, puncture several holes in the back of each crab (this will keep crabs from exploding when fried). Recoat crabs with flour mixture.

Heat oil in a large saucepan over medium-high heat to 350° F. Deep-fry crabs, 2 at a time, until golden brown, about 3 to 4 minutes. Drain on paper towels. Set 2 crabs at side of each of 4 serving plates and keep warm.

For sauce, heat olive oil in a medium skillet over high heat. Add onions, garlic, and ginger and sauté until lightly browned, about 2 minutes. Add stock, soy sauce, lemon juice, bell pepper, bean sauce, and Thai seasoning and cook, stirring 2 to 3 minutes. Pour ¼ of the sauce over the other side of each serving plate, garnish with mint, and serve.

MALAYSIAN CLAMS

You'll want to lick your plate, this sauce is so tasty. Use Manila clams if you can get them; they're especially tender and flavorful.

6 TABLESPOONS OLIVE OIL

2 TABLESPOONS FINELY CHOPPED RED ONIONS

1 TABLESPOON FINELY CHOPPED GARLIC

2½ POUNDS MANILA CLAMS OR LITTLENECK CLAMS, SCRUBBED

16 DRIED WHOLE CHILIES

1½ TABLESPOONS ROASTED CHILI PASTE

1 CUP SLICED ONIONS

½ CUP DICED RED BELL PEPPER

½ CUP LEMON GRASS STOCK OR CHICKEN STOCK (SEE PAGE 110)

¼ CUP RED BELL PEPPER PUREE (SEE PAGE 111)

2 TABLESPOONS OYSTER SAUCE

2 TABLESPOONS CHOPPED THAI OR REGULAR BASIL

1 TABLESPOON THAI SWEET BLACK BEAN SAUCE

2 TEASPOONS THAI FISH SAUCE

2 TEASPOONS MAGGI SAUCE (OPTIONAL)

2 TEASPOONS BLACK PEPPER

4 SPRIGS BASIL (GARNISH)

Heat olive oil in a large deep skillet over high heat. Add chopped onions and garlic and sauté until lightly browned, about 1½ minutes. Add clams, dried chilies, and chili paste and cook, stirring constantly, 2 minutes. Add sliced onions, bell pepper, stock, pepper puree, oyster sauce, chopped basil, bean sauce, fish sauce, Maggi sauce, and black pepper and cook, stirring constantly, until clams open, about 3 minutes; discard any unopened clams. Transfer clams to a platter, garnish with basil, and serve.

Santa Fe Chili Mussels

I learned about Santa Fe chili powder from my friend John Sedlar, chef/owner of the Saint Estephe restaurant in Manhatttan Beach, California. John, a native of Santa Fe, introduced me to a family who grow the chilies and prepared a few dishes for me using the powder. It was love at first bite; I couldn't wait to get into the kitchen to create some new dishes with it.

6 TABLESPOONS OLIVE OIL

2 TABLESPOONS FINELY CHOPPED RED ONIONS

1 TABLESPOON FINELY CHOPPED GARLIC

1 TABLESPOON FINELY CHOPPED, PEELED FRESH GINGER

4 POUNDS NEW ZEALAND OR BLACK MUSSELS, SCRUBBED AND DEBEARDED

16 WHOLE DRIED CHILIES

1 TABLESPOON ROASTED CHILI PASTE

2 TEASPOONS SANTA FE CHILI POWDER

1 CUP SLICED ONIONS

½ CUP LEMON GRASS STOCK OR CHICKEN STOCK (SEE PAGE 110)

½ CUP DICED RED BELL PEPPER

¼ CUP CHOPPED THAI OR REGULAR BASIL

¼ CUP RED BELL PEPPER PUREE (SEE PAGE 111)

¼ CUP TOMATO PUREE (SEE PAGE 111)

1 ½ TABLESPOONS THAI FISH SAUCE

2 TEASPOONS MAGGI SAUCE (OPTIONAL)

4 SPRIGS BASIL (GARNISH)

Heat olive oil in a large deep skillet over high heat. Add chopped onions, garlic, and ginger and sauté until garlic is lightly browned, about 1½ minutes. Add mussels, dried chilies, chili paste, and chili powder and cook, stirring constantly, 2 minutes. Add sliced onions, stock, bell pepper, chopped basil, pepper puree, tomato puree, fish sauce, and Maggi sauce and cook, stirring constantly, until mussels open about 4 minutes; discard any mussels that do not open. Transfer to a large platter, garnish with basil, and serve.

OYSTERS WITH GINGER SAUCE

One of the many Thai recipes that use Chinese oyster sauce. This is easy to fix but makes a real company dish.

¼ CUP OLIVE OIL

2 TEASPOONS FINELY CHOPPED GARLIC

¼ CUP THINLY SLICED, PEELED FRESH GINGER

1 TEASPOON FINELY CHOPPED SERRANO CHILI

24 LARGE OYSTERS, SHUCKED AND RINSED

16 SHIITAKE MUSHROOMS

½ CUP SLICED ONIONS

½ CUP DICED LEEKS

¼ CUP CHICKEN STOCK (SEE PAGE 110)

2 TABLESPOONS OYSTER SAUCE

1 TABLESPOON THAI FISH SAUCE

2 TEASPOONS THAI SWEET BLACK BEAN SAUCE

1 TEASPOON BLACK PEPPER

1 SMALL PACKET ENOKI MUSHROOMS (GARNISH)

Heat olive oil in a large skillet over high heat. Add garlic and sauté until lightly browned, about 1 minute. Add ginger and serrano chili and sauté 1 minute. Add oysters and cook, stirring, 2 minutes. Add shiitake mushrooms, onions, leaks, stock, oyster sauce, fish sauce, black bean sauce, and pepper and cook, stirring constantly, 3 minutes. Transfer to a platter, surround with enoki mushrooms, and serve.

ROASTED CHILI OYSTERS

I fixed this dish for a celebrity party once. I'd always assumed that movie stars don't eat a lot, but they practically inhaled these oysters. I would have needed ten arms to keep up with them.

½ CUP ALL-PURPOSE FLOUR

1 TABLESPOON CURRY POWDER

24 LARGE OYSTERS, SHUCKED AND RINSED (RESERVE SHELLS)

¼ CUP OLIVE OIL

3 TABLESPOONS UNSALTED BUTTER

¼ CUP OLIVE OIL

2 TABLESPOONS FINELY CHOPPED SHALLOTS

1 TABLESPOON FINELY CHOPPED GARLIC

1½ TABLESPOONS ROASTED CHILI PASTE

1 TABLESPOON FINELY CHOPPED KAFFIR LIME LEAVES

1 TABLESPOON FINELY CHOPPED FRESH LEMON GRASS (THICKER BASE OF STALK ONLY, 3 OUTER LAYERS REMOVED)

½ CUP COCONUT MILK (SEE PAGE 112)

¼ CUP WHIPPED CREAM

1 TABLESPOON SHRIMP POWDER

1 TABLESPOON THAI FISH SAUCE

1 TABLESPOON THINLY SLICED KAFFIR LIME LEAVES (GARNISH)

Combine flour and curry powder in a large bowl and mix well. Add oysters and toss gently to coat; remove and shake off excess. Heat ¼ cup olive oil with butter in a large skillet over medium heat. Add oysters and sauté until crisp and browned on all sides, about 3 minutes. Replace oysters in shells and arrange on serving plates.

Heat ¼ cup olive oil in a medium skillet over high heat. Add shallots and garlic and sauté until lightly browned, about 1½ minutes. Add chili paste, lime leaves, and lemon grass and cook, stirring constantly, 2 minutes. Add coconut milk, whipped cream, shrimp powder, and fish sauce and cook, stirring constantly, 3 minutes. Top each oyster with a dab of sauce, garnish with lime leaves, and serve.

SCALLOPS WITH MANGO SALSA

This dish is so light and refreshing, you'll feel thinner even before you start to eat. It is simple to prepare so don't give up if you cannot find the mango. Just replace it with sour green apple and put your Jane Fonda workout tape away.

¼ CUP OLIVE OIL

1 ½ TABLESPOONS TOMMY TANG'S THAI
    SEASONING

2 POUNDS EXTRA-LARGE SEA SCALLOPS
    (8 TO 10 PER POUND)

4 10-INCH SPRIGS ROSEMARY OR
    BAMBOO SKEWERS

MANGO SALSA (SEE PAGE 39)

Combine olive oil and Thai seasoning in a mixing bowl and whisk to blend. Add scallops and toss gently to coat well. Cover bowl with plastic wrap and refrigerate 3 hours.

Prepare charcoal grill. Strip leaves from rosemary sprigs to make "skewers," or substitute bamboo skewers. Thread scallops on skewers, dividing evenly. Grill 3 minutes on each side. (Alternatively, heat 2 teaspoons olive oil in a large skillet over high heat; add scallops and sauté 2 to 3 minutes on each side.) Place 1 skewer on each of 4 serving plates, spoon salsa onto other side of plate, and serve.

Sunrise Scallops with Ginger Cream Sauce and Chili "Flames"

When a Japanese friend came to visit I wanted to make him feel welcome, so I created this dish in honor of the Japanese flag, which depicts a bright red sun.

¼ CUP OLIVE OIL

2 TABLESPOONS TOMMY TANG'S THAI SEASONING

2 POUNDS EXTRA-LARGE SEA SCALLOPS (8 TO 10 PER POUND)

1½ TEASPOONS SANTA FE CHILI POWDER

GINGER CREAM SAUCE

2 TABLESPOONS UNSALTED BUTTER

2 TABLESPOONS OLIVE OIL

2 TABLESPOONS FINELY CHOPPED SHALLOTS

2 TABLESPOONS FINELY CHOPPED GARLIC

¼ CUP FINELY CHOPPED, PEELED FRESH GINGER

½ CUP DRY WHITE WINE

1 TABLESPOON THAI FISH SAUCE

2 TEASPOONS WHITE PEPPER

¾ CUP COCONUT MILK (SEE PAGE 112)

1¼ CUPS WHIPPING CREAM

SANTA FE CHILI "FLAMES"

⅓ CUP GINGER CREAM SAUCE (SEE RECIPE ABOVE)

2 TEASPOONS SANTA FE CHILI POWDER

Combine ¼ cup olive oil and Thai seasoning in a large mixing bowl and whisk to blend well. Add scallops and toss gently until completely coated. Cover bowl with plastic wrap and refrigerate 3 hours.

Prepare charcoal grill. Grill scallops until opaque, about 3 minutes on each side. Or, alternatively, place a large skillet over high heat. Coat it with 1 tablespoon olive oil, add scallops, and sear for 2 to 3 minutes on each side. Arrange on paper towels to absorb excess liquid. Sprinkle with 1½ teaspoons chili powder and set aside.

For sauce, melt butter with oil in a deep saucepan over high heat. Add shallots and garlic and sauté 2 minutes. Add ginger and sauté, stirring, 2 minutes. Add wine, fish sauce, and white pepper and bring to boil, then reduce heat to medium and cook, stirring, 3 minutes. Add coconut milk, increase heat to high, and bring to boil; boil 2 minutes. Stir in cream and return to boil. Reduce heat to low and simmer until reduced by half, about 5 minutes. Strain sauce through a fine sieve and keep warm.

For chili "flames," combine 1/3 cup ginger cream sauce and chili powder in a small squeeze bottle and shake well to blend.

Divide ginger cream sauce among 4 serving plates, smoothing over entire bottom of plate. Arrange a cluster of scallops in center of each plate. Squeeze straight lines of chili mixture around scallops and gently stroke across lines with tines of fork to make "flames." Serve right away.

Blackened Scallops with Roasted Garlic Chili Sauce

Using a base of roasted chili paste, this sauce is simple to make. Get a couple of extra jars of the paste—you'll find yourself running out of it sooner than you'd think.

¼ CUP OLIVE OIL

2 TABLESPOONS TOMMY TANG'S THAI SEASONING

2 POUNDS EXTRA-LARGE SEA SCALLOPS (8 TO 10 PER POUND)

1 TABLESPOON OLIVE OIL

ROASTED GARLIC CHILI SAUCE
3 TABLESPOONS OLIVE OIL

2 TABLESPOONS FINELY CHOPPED GARLIC

1 TABLESPOON FINELY CHOPPED, PEELED FRESH GINGER

1 TABLESPOON ROASTED CHILI PASTE

½ CUP COCONUT MILK (SEE PAGE 112)

1 TABLESPOON THAI FISH SAUCE

⅓ CUP WHIPPING CREAM

4 SPRIGS MINT (GARNISH)

Combine ¼ cup olive oil and Thai seasoning in a large bowl and mix well. Add scallops and toss gently to coat. Cover bowl with plastic wrap and refrigerate 3 hours.

Heat 1 tablespoon olive oil in a large skillet over high heat. Add scallops and cook just until blackened, about 3 to 4 minutes on each side. Transfer to paper towels to absorb excess juice; set aside and keep warm.

For sauce, heat olive oil in a medium saucepan over high heat. Add garlic and sauté until lightly browned, about 1½ minutes. Add ginger and chili paste and cook, stirring, 1 minute. Add coconut milk and fish sauce and bring to boil, stirring constantly. Reduce heat to medium and cook until sauce is reduced by half, about 2 to 3 minutes. Add cream and return to boil. Reduce heat to low and simmer until slightly thickened, 3 to 4 minutes. Strain sauce through a fine sieve.

Smooth sauce over bottoms of 4 serving plates. Arrange scallops in center of sauce, garnish with mint, and serve.

SPICY GARLIC SHRIMP

Similar to Italian scampi, but spicier—and to me this tastes better.

6 TABLESPOONS OLIVE OIL

¼ CUP FINELY CHOPPED RED ONIONS

3 TABLESPOONS FINELY CHOPPED GARLIC

1 TEASPOON FINELY CHOPPED SERRANO CHILI

20 LARGE SHRIMP (13 TO 15 PER POUND), SHELLED AND DEVEINED

1 TABLESPOON BLACK PEPPER

¾ CUP LEMON GRASS STOCK (SEE PAGE 110)

½ CUP TOMATO PUREE (SEE PAGE 111)

2 TABLESPOONS FINELY DICED RED BELL PEPPER

1 TABLESPOON THAI FISH SAUCE

1 TABLESPOON THAI SWEET BLACK BEAN SAUCE

1 TEASPOON MAGGI SAUCE (OPTIONAL)

4 SPRIGS MINT (GARNISH)

Heat olive oil in a large skillet over high heat. Add onions, garlic, and serrano chili and sauté until garlic is lightly browned, about 2 minutes. Add shrimp and black pepper and sauté, stirring constantly, 3 minutes. Add lemon grass stock, tomato puree, bell pepper, fish sauce, bean sauce, and Maggi sauce and cook, stirring constantly, 2 minutes. Transfer to a platter, garnish with mint, and serve.

PRIK KING SHRIMP

Prik means "chili" in Thai. When I first arrived in the United States I went to the supermarket with my roommate, who had come here from Thailand a few years earlier. I asked him to get some prik; he nearly dropped dead on the spot, and everyone within six feet turned to stare at me.

6 TABLESPOONS OLIVE OIL

1 TABLESPOON FINELY CHOPPED GARLIC

2 TEASPOONS FINELY CHOPPED, PEELED FRESH GINGER

1 CUP COCONUT MILK (SEE PAGE 112)

1 ½ TABLESPOONS THAI RED CURRY PASTE

2 TEASPOONS PAPRIKA

24 MEDIUM SHRIMP (21 TO 25 PER POUND), SHELLED AND DEVEINED

2 CUPS GREEN BEANS CUT INTO 1 ½-INCH-LONG JULIENNE

½ CUP DICED RED BELL PEPPER

1 ½ TABLESPOONS GROUND UNSALTED PEANUTS

1 TABLESPOON THAI FISH SAUCE

1 TABLESPOON SHRIMP POWDER

1 TABLESPOON THINLY SLICED KAFFIR LIME LEAVES, OR SUBSTITUTE LEMON LEAVES

1 TEASPOON SUGAR (OPTIONAL)

4 SPRIGS BASIL (GARNISH)

Heat olive oil in a large skillet over high heat. Add garlic and ginger and sauté until lightly browned, about 1½ minutes. Add coconut milk, curry paste, and paprika and cook, stirring constantly, 2 minutes. Add shrimp, beans, bell pepper, peanuts, fish sauce, shrimp powder, lime leaves, and sugar and cook, stirring constantly, until shrimp are cooked through, 4 to 5 minutes. Transfer to a platter, garnish with basil, and serve.

Shrimp and Asparagus with Roasted Chili Sauce

Once you start to experiment with roasted chili paste you will find yourself running out of it in no time. Just force your local gourmet market to carry it! The dried chilies in this dish are optional—and strictly for daredevils.

6 TABLESPOONS OLIVE OIL

2 TABLESPOONS FINELY CHOPPED RED ONIONS

2 TABLESPOONS FINELY CHOPPED GARLIC

24 RAW MEDIUM SHRIMP (21 TO 25 PER POUND), SHELLED AND DEVEINED

2 ½ CUPS TRIMMED ASPARAGUS CUT INTO 2-INCH LENGTHS

1 ½ TABLESPOONS ROASTED CHILI PASTE

12 DRIED SMALL WHOLE CHILIES (OPTIONAL)

½ CUP RED BELL PEPPER PUREE (SEE PAGE 111)

½ CUP DICED RED BELL PEPPER

½ CUP DICED ONIONS

½ CUP LEMON GRASS STOCK OR CHICKEN STOCK (SEE PAGE 110)

1 TABLESPOON THAI FISH SAUCE

1 TABLESPOON THAI SWEET BLACK BEAN SAUCE

1 TEASPOON BLACK PEPPER

Heat olive oil in a large skillet over high heat. Add red onions and garlic and sauté until lightly browned, about 1½ minutes. Add shrimp, asparagus, chili paste, and whole chilies and cook, stirring constantly, 2 minutes. Add all remaining ingredients and cook, stirring constantly, 3 more minutes. Transfer to a platter and serve.

TIGER PRAWNS WITH CILANTRO CREAM SAUCE

Yes, this dish is expensive, so prepare it when you're inviting someone special, such as your mother-in-law or the boss, whom you're going to ask to move you into a larger office. Even if you don't get the new office, you'll certainly endear yourself to your boss.

12 TIGER PRAWNS (6 TO 8 PER POUND), IN SHELLS

⅓ CUP OLIVE OIL

3 TABLESPOONS TOMMY TANG'S THAI SEASONING

2 TABLESPOONS UNSALTED BUTTER

2 TABLESPOONS OLIVE OIL

3 TABLESPOONS FINELY CHOPPED RED ONIONS

2 TABLESPOONS FINELY CHOPPED GARLIC

1 CUP COCONUT MILK (SEE PAGE 112)

½ CUP FINELY CHOPPED CILANTRO

½ CUP WHIPPING CREAM

1 TABLESPOON THAI FISH SAUCE

1½ TEASPOONS WHITE PEPPER

4 SPRIGS CILANTRO (GARNISH)

Using poultry shears, make a shallow lengthwise cut along the back of each prawn, leaving shell on. Remove intestinal vein and rinse prawns with cold water. Pat dry with paper towels. Combine ⅓ cup olive oil and Thai seasoning in a large bowl, add prawns, and toss to coat well.

Insert a 10-inch metal or bamboo skewer lengthwise in each prawn, starting at the tail end, to keep it straight during grilling. Place prawns in a square container, pour left-over marinade over the prawns, cover, and refrigerate 3 hours.

Prepare charcoal grill, or preheat oven broiler. Melt butter with 2 tablespoons olive oil in a medium saucepan over high heat. Add onions and garlic and sauté until lightly browned, about 2 minutes. Add coconut milk and cilantro and bring to boil, stirring constantly. Boil for 2 minutes. Add whipping cream, fish sauce, and white pepper. Bring sauce to boil again, then reduce heat to low and simmer until sauce is reduced by half, about 4 to 5 minutes. Strain through a fine sieve and keep warm.

While sauce is simmering, charcoal-grill prawns just until cooked through, about 5 to 6 minutes on each side. Or place prawns, coated with leftover marinade, on a thick pan. Wrap bamboo skewers with aluminum foil, leaving only the prawns exposed, and broil for 6 to 8 minutes without turning. Remove skewers from prawns. Arrange 3 prawns in a circle on each serving plate. Pour ¼ of sauce in center of each plate, garnish with cilantro, and serve.

M E A T

Grilled Fillet of Beef

You'll find your friends and neighbors dropping by more often if you let them taste this; serve it to your mother-in-law and she'll forgive you for forgetting to buy her a Mother's Day gift.

MARINADE

½ CUP OLIVE OIL

¼ CUP ASIAN SESAME OIL

¼ CUP SOY SAUCE

2 TABLESPOONS SUGAR OR HONEY

2 TABLESPOONS THAI SWEET BLACK BEAN SAUCE

2 TABLESPOONS GRANULATED GARLIC

1 TABLESPOON BLACK PEPPER

1 ½ TEASPOONS FINELY CHOPPED GARLIC

1 TEASPOON PAPRIKA

2 POUNDS BEEF TENDERLOIN

1 SMALL PINEAPPLE

SWEET CHILI SAUCE (SEE PAGE 82)

Combine marinade ingredients in a large bowl and whisk until thick and well blended.

Cut beef on the bias into slices ¼ inch thick and 4 to 5 inches long. Add to marinade and rub gently to coat all surfaces. Cover bowl with plastic wrap and refrigerate at least 6 hours, preferably overnight.

Cut pineapple into 4 lengthwise wedges. On each wedge, cut in at an angle on each side of core, then slide knife under core and remove it.

Prepare charcoal grill. Grill meat to desired doneness, about 2 to 2½ minutes on each side for medium, 5 to 6 minutes for well done. (Alternatively, cook in a large skillet over high heat, in batches if necessary, for 3 minutes on each side.) Transfer to a platter and serve with pineapple wedges and sweet chili sauce.

Spicy Pork Chops with Thai Chili Fish Sauce

Do you think a pork chop is a pork chop? Wait until you taste these. Serve them with Thai Papaya Salad (see page 40). If you prefer a less spicy sauce, substitute the Sweet Chili Sauce on page 82.

MARINADE

¼ CUP OLIVE OIL

¼ CUP HONEY

¼ CUP FINELY CHOPPED GARLIC

3 TABLESPOONS THAI SWEET BLACK BEAN SAUCE

2 TABLESPOONS THAI FISH SAUCE

2 TABLESPOONS FINELY CHOPPED CILANTRO

1 TABLESPOON GRANULATED GARLIC

2 TEASPOONS FINELY CHOPPED SERRANO CHILI

2 TEASPOONS GROUND CORIANDER

2 TEASPOONS BLACK PEPPER

2 TEASPOONS WHITE PEPPER

8 ¾-INCH-THICK PORK CHOPS

THAI CHILI FISH SAUCE

6 TABLESPOONS THAI FISH SAUCE

5 TABLESPOONS THINLY SLICED SCALLIONS

3 TABLESPOONS FRESH LIME JUICE OR LEMON JUICE

3 TABLESPOONS FINELY CHOPPED CILANTRO

1 ½ TABLESPOONS FINELY CHOPPED SERRANO CHILI

2 TEASPOONS ROASTED CHILI PASTE

½ TEASPOON FINELY CHOPPED GARLIC

Combine all marinade ingredients in a large bowl and whisk to blend well. Add pork chops and rub gently to coat. Cover bowl with plastic wrap and refrigerate at least 6 hours, preferably overnight.

For chili fish sauce, combine all ingredients in a small bowl and mix well.

Prepare charcoal grill. Grill pork chops about 7 minutes on each side. (Alternatively, bake in preheated 375° F. oven for 12 to 14 minutes.) Divide chops among 4 serving plates. Serve sauce with chops.

Rosemary Baby Lamb with Curry Yogurt Sauce

Thais aren't usually fond of lamb, so I once had to fool a Thai friend by telling him these were pork chops. He ate twice as much as I did. The cool sauce makes a very pleasant contrast with the sizzling grilled lamb chops.

1 CUP COCONUT MILK (SEE PAGE 112)

2 TABLESPOONS POWDERED ROSEMARY

2 TABLESPOONS CHOPPED GARLIC

1 TABLESPOON THAI FISH SAUCE

1 TABLESPOON THAI SWEET
  BLACK BEAN SAUCE

1 TABLESPOON CURRY POWDER

2 TEASPOONS WHITE PEPPER

2 TEASPOONS BLACK PEPPER

1 TEASPOON CHOPPED SERRANO CHILI

12 ¾-INCH-THICK BABY LAMB CHOPS

CURRY YOGURT SAUCE

2 TABLESPOONS VIRGIN OLIVE OIL

1 CUP LOW-FAT PLAIN YOGURT

4 6-INCH SPRIGS ROSEMARY (GARNISH)

Combine coconut milk, powdered rosemary, garlic, fish sauce, bean sauce, curry powder, white and black pepper, and serrano chili in a large bowl and whisk to blend well. Add lamb chops and rub gently with marinade to coat on all sides. Cover bowl with plastic wrap and refrigerate at least 6 hours, preferably overnight. Drain lamb, reserving marinade.

Heat olive oil in a medium skillet over medium heat. Add reserved marinade mixture and cook, stirring constantly, 3 minutes. Strain through a fine sieve, reserving 1 tablespoon; discard remainder. Combine reserved strained sauce with yogurt in a medium bowl and whisk gently to blend.

Prepare charcoal grill or preheat oven to 400° F. Grill chops about 3 minutes on each side, or bake 5 to 7 minutes without turning. The chops will be cooked through but still moist and pink inside. Place 3 chops to 1 side of each of 4 serving plates. Spoon yogurt sauce onto opposite side of plate, garnish with rosemary, and serve.

BASIC RECIPES

Chicken Stock

MAKES ABOUT 6 CUPS

12 CUPS WATER

3 POUNDS MEATY CHICKEN BONES

1 CUP CELERY CHUNKS

1 CUP CARROT CHUNKS

1 WHOLE ONION, PEELED

Bring water to boil in a stockpot over high heat. Add all remaining ingredients and return to boil, then reduce heat to medium and boil until reduced by half, about 1 hour and 20 minutes. Strain stock and let cool, then remove all fat from surface. Refrigerate for up to a week; freeze for longer storage.

Lemon Grass Stock

MAKES ABOUT 6 CUPS

6 CUPS CHICKEN STOCK (SEE PREVIOUS RECIPE)

6 PIECES DRIED GALANGA

2 STALKS LEMON GRASS, PREFERABLY FRESH

Combine all ingredients in a medium stockpot and bring to boil over high heat. Reduce heat to low and simmer 15 minutes, skimming any fat that rises to the surface. Strain.

Red or Green Bell Pepper Puree

MAKES ABOUT 2 CUPS

6 LARGE RED OR GREEN BELL PEPPERS

1 TEASPOON FINELY CHOPPED GARLIC

Roast peppers on gas burner or under broiler until blistered on all sides, turning frequently. Transfer to a plastic bag, close bag, and let stand at least 15 minutes. Peel and seed peppers under cold running water; drain.

Puree peppers in a food processor or blender. Transfer puree to a small saucepan, add garlic, and bring to boil over high heat. Reduce heat to low and simmer 10 minutes; cool. Puree can be kept in refrigerator up to 3 days; freeze for longer storage.

Tomato Puree

MAKES ABOUT 2½ CUPS

6 CUPS WATER

6 LARGE TOMATOES

1 TEASPOON FINELY CHOPPED GARLIC

Bring water to boil in a large saucepan over high heat. Cut shallow cross in stem end of each tomato. Drop tomatoes into boiling water and blanch 2 minutes, then immediately drain and place in a large bowl of ice water to stop cooking process. Peel and seed tomatoes.

Puree tomatoes in a food processor or blender. Transfer puree to a small saucepan, add garlic, and bring to boil over high heat. Reduce heat to low and simmer 15 minutes; cool. Puree can be kept in refrigerator up to 3 days; freeze for longer storage.

Coconut Milk

MAKES ABOUT 5 CUPS
6 CUPS BOILING WATER

3 CUPS DRIED, UNSWEETENED FLAKED
COCONUT

Combine water and coconut in a large bowl and mix well. Set aside until cooled to lukewarm. Transfer about ¼ of mixture to a blender and puree at high speed 1 minute.

Line a stainer with 2 layers of dampened cheesecloth. Pour pureed coconut mixture through strainer into a medium saucepan. Gather corners of cheesecloth and squeeze as much liquid as possible into saucepan. Repeat blending and straining steps with remaining coconut mixture.

Place saucepan over medium heat and bring just to boiling point, then remove from heat and let cool. Coconut milk can be kept in refrigerator up to 2 days; freeze for longer storage.

Tamarind Juice

Tamarind paste is ordinarily sold in 8-ounce packages; each package will make 4 batches of Tamarind Juice.

MAKES ABOUT 2 CUPS
2 CUPS COLD WATER

¼ CUP TAMARIND PASTE

Combine water and tamarind paste in a medium bowl and squeeze with your hands until paste loosens and disperses through water, about 2 minutes. Let stand 20 minutes, then strain through a fine sieve. Tamarind juice can be kept in refrigerator up to 3 days; freeze for longer storage.

1. PANANG CURRY PASTE
2. KRA-CHAI
3. CORIANDER SEEDS
4. TAMARIND
5. GREEN CURRY PASTE
6. CARDAMOM SEEDS
7. DRIED CHILI PEPPER
8. CUMIN SEEDS
9. CLOVES
10. RED CURRY PASTE
11. STAR ANISE
12. JAPANESE HORSERADISH (WASABI)
13. CURRY POWDER
14. THAI MUSSAMUN CURRY PASTE
15. SANTA FE CHILI POWDER
16. CINNAMON STICK
17. DRIED GALANGA
18. FRESH CHILI PASTE (SAMBAL OELEK)

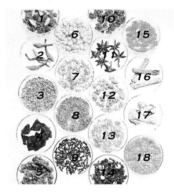

1. THAI SAUSAGE
2. DRIED SHRIMP POWDER
3. FIRM BROWN TOFU
4. SEAWEED
5. FRESH RICE NOODLES
6. PAD THAI NOODLES (SEN CHAN)
7. GRANULATED COCONUT
8. MEEKROB NOODLES (SEN-MEE)
9. BLACK AND WHITE PEPPERCORNS
10. PALM SUGAR
11. PLUM SAUCE
12. BEAN CONDIMENT
13. STRIP BAMBOO

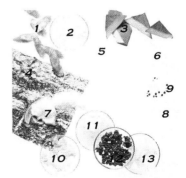

THE ORIGINAL TOMMY DUCK WITH HONEY GINGER SAUCE [p. 80]

Spicy BBQ Chicken with Sweet Chili Sauce [p. 82]

GRILLED RED SNAPPER WITH ROSEMARY HONEY GLAZE [p. 89]

SIAMESE CHICKEN WITH BASIL [p. 86]

ROASTED CHILI OYSTERS [p. 96]

SUNRISE SCALLOPS WITH GINGER CREAM SAUCE AND CHILI "FLAMES" [*p. 98*]

ROSEMARY BABY LAMB WITH CURRY YOGURT SAUCE [p. 107]

Cooked White or Brown Rice

The easiest and most foolproof way to cook rice is in an electric rice cooker; it does a perfect job and lets you know when the rice is done. If you're not lucky enough to own an automatic cooker, here's my method for preparing rice on top of the stove.

MAKES ABOUT 4 CUPS

4 CUPS (FOR WHITE RICE) OR 6 CUPS (FOR BROWN RICE) HOT WATER

1 ⅓ CUPS LONG-GRAIN WHITE OR BROWN RICE, RINSED IN COLD WATER

Combine water and rice in a medium saucepan and bring to boil over high heat. Reduce heat to medium and cook until rice grains are swollen, about 15 to 17 minutes for white rice or 23 to 25 minutes for brown (to test for doneness, squeeze a grain of rice between your fingernails; if there is no hard, white spot at the center, the rice is cooked). Transfer rice to strainer and drain well. Cover and keep warm.

Sushi Rice

How to cook Sushi Rice is a subject that often comes up when I chat with customers at our sushi bar. They are all either afraid to cook the rice at home or disappointed with the results when they do. I hope this recipe will make things easier for those who want to try again. As with the basic rice recipe above, an electric rice cooker does a foolproof job.

MAKES ABOUT 4 CUPS
4 CUPS HOT WATER
1 CUP JAPANESE SHORT-GRAIN RICE,
   RINSED IN COLD WATER

2 TABLESPOONS SUSHI RICE STOCK
   (RECIPE FOLLOWS)

Combine water and rice in a medium saucepan and bring to boil over high heat. Reduce heat to medium and cook until rice grains are swollen, about 15 to 17 minutes (to test for doneness, squeeze a grain of rice between your fingernails; if there is no hard, white spot at the center, the rice is cooked). Transfer rice to a strainer and drain well.

Transfer cooked rice to large bowl, add sushi rice stock, and mix well with a spatula. Cool to lukewarm, then use in preparing sushi.

SUSHI RICE STOCK

At my restaurant we make this in batches large enough to last up to a month. You can halve this recipe if you're not anticipating much sushi-making, and any extra stock can be frozen.

MAKES ABOUT 2 ½ CUPS

1 ½ CUPS RICE VINEGAR

1 CUP WATER

¼ CUP SAKE

2 TABLESPOONS SUGAR

½ TEASPOON SALT

Combine all ingredients in a nonaluminum medium saucepan and bring to boil over high heat. Reduce heat to low and simmer 15 minutes. Let cool. Stock can be kept in refrigerator for 4 weeks; freeze for longer storage.

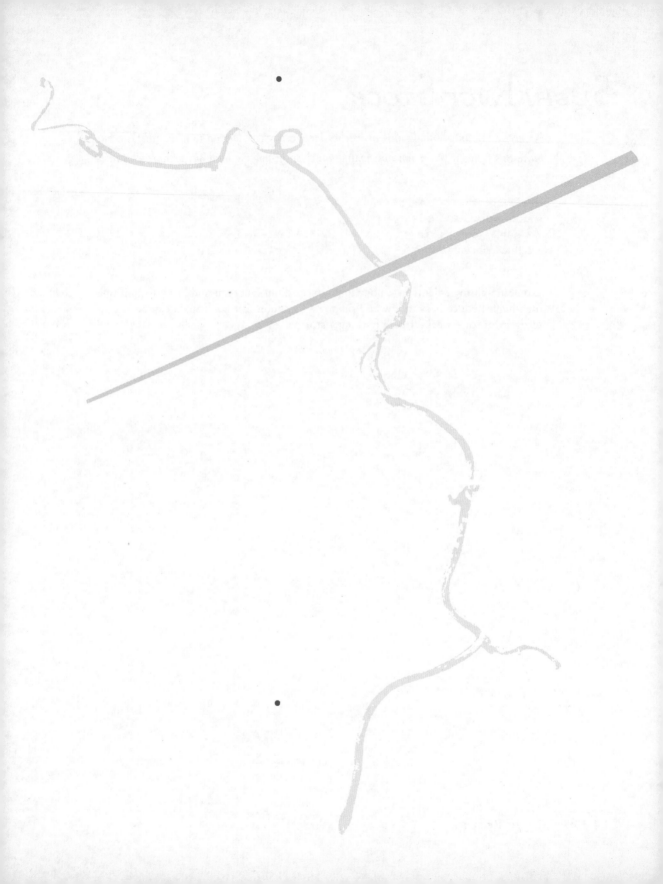

SUGGESTED MENUS

SUGGESTED DINNER PARTY MENUS

Cooking a dinner for friends or family—from 4 to 12 people—doesn't have to be difficult. These seasonal menu suggestions are intended to make life easier; just select 1 dish for each course. Naturally these are only guidelines; feel free to add, subtract, or substitute dishes as you wish. Thai people generally eat from communal bowls and platters, with all the food served at once. I find this an enjoyable custom that stimulates conversation, but you may prefer to serve in successive courses, Western-style—it's up to you. I haven't included recipes for sweets in this book, so don't forget dessert if you like it—maybe a selection of fresh fruit, tropical or otherwise.

S P R I N G

FIRST COURSE:

Meekrob
California Roll
Crab Spring Rolls with Santa Fe Chili Yogurt Sauce
Nam Chicken

SECOND COURSE:

Arugula Salad with Rosemary Honey Vinaigrette
Thai Papaya Salad
Malaysian Clams
Soft-Shell Crabs with Garlic Ginger Sauce

THIRD COURSE:

Thai Pasta
Seafood Pasta with Curry Cream Sauce
Spicy Mint Fried Rice
Pineapple Fried Rice

FOURTH COURSE:

Scallops with Mango Salsa
Grilled Salmon with Kaffir Lime Sauce
Lemon Grass Chicken
Shrimp Panang

SUMMER

FIRST COURSE:

Mussel Sate with Ginger Cream Sauce
Spicy Tuna Roll
Thai Toast
King Cobra

SECOND COURSE:

Thai Sausage Salad
Thai Eggplant
Mango Salsa
Santa Fe Chili Mussels

THIRD COURSE:

Pad Thai
Chicken Noodles Alfonse
Curry Fried Rice
Brunei Egg Crepes

FOURTH COURSE:

Spicy BBQ Chicken with Sweet Chili Sauce
Grilled Red Snapper with Rosemary Honey Glaze
Lamb Mussamun
Sunrise Scallops with Ginger Cream Sauce and Chili "Flames"

F A L L

FIRST COURSE:

Chicken Sate with Peanut Sauce
Tiger's Eye
Larb
Thai Egg Rolls or Thai Wonton

SECOND COURSE:

Tom Yum Kung or Tom Kha Kai
Warm Spinach Chicken Salad
Naked Shrimp Salad
Roasted Chili Oysters

THIRD COURSE:

Lard-Na Noodles
Santa Fe Chili Pasta
Duck Fried Rice
Vegetarian Noodles

FOURTH COURSE:

Original Tommy's Duck with Honey Ginger Sauce
Tiger Prawns with Cilantro Cream Sauce
Blackened Scallops with Roasted Garlic Chili Sauce
Spicy Pork Chops with Thai Chili Fish Sauce

WINTER

FIRST COURSE:

Volcanic Mussels
Spicy Wonton with Sweet Tamarind Sauce
Angel Wings
Manhattan Roll

SECOND COURSE:

Tom Kha Kai or Tom Yum Kung
Spicy Beef Salad with Lemon Grass Sauce
Santa Fe Chili Mussels
Spicy Garlic Mushrooms

THIRD COURSE:

Panang Curry Pasta with Pine Nuts and Basil
Spicy Mint Noodles
Black Olive Fried Rice
Bangkok Jambalaya

FOURTH COURSE:

Rosemary Baby Lamb with Curry Yogurt Sauce
Thai Chili Fish
Siamese Chicken with Basil
Alaska King Crab Curry

SUGGESTED COCKTAIL PARTY MENUS

Planning a cocktail party—which may be for 10 people, or for 100 or more —is not a simple task. You want your guests to be entertained, to be comfortable, and to be able to mingle easily and enjoy themselves. Selecting the menu is the most important part of the planning; bite-size finger foods, which can be presented on trays and which don't require utensils or plates, are ideal.

Selecting 3 to 5 items from this list will make your party the talk of the town. We've served these dishes from Oscar night in Hollywood to Tony Awards night in New York—and always with huge success.

California Roll

Chicken Sate with Peanut Sauce

Crab Spring Rolls with
    Santa Fe Chili Yogurt Sauce

Manhattan Roll

Spicy Tuna Roll

Mussel Sate with Ginger Cream Sauce

Roasted Chili Oysters

Spicy Wonton with Sweet Tamarind Sauce

Thai Egg Rolls

Thai Toast

Thai Wonton

Tiger's Eye

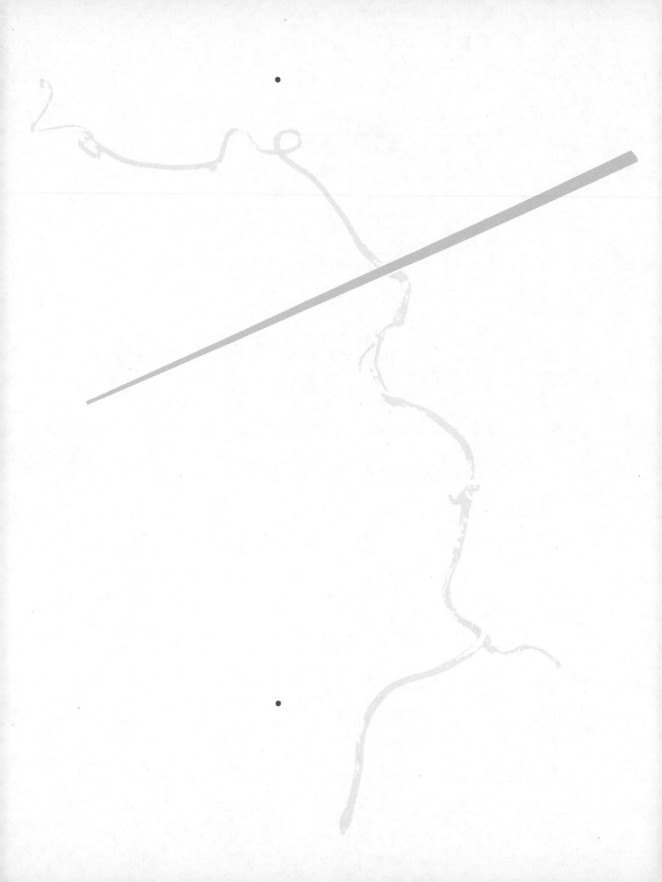

Sources for Ingredients

ABOUT THAI/ASIAN INGREDIENTS

Many of the Thai and Asian ingredients mentioned in this book are found in many supermarkets and specialty food shops throughout North America. To purchase ingredients online, visit www.letsgetcooking.org. At this website, you can also learn about Tommy Tang's PBS Cooking Series.

THE TSUNAMI CHILDREN FOUNDATION

Overwhelmed by the tragic loss of life in Thailand after the devastating tsunami of December 2004, Tommy Tang, like so many others, wanted to do something to help. A trip to Thailand in the wake of this tragic event inspired Tommy to immediately establish the Tsunami Children Foundation.

The main purpose of this nonprofit organization is to provide psychological care to those people of Thailand who were affected by the tsunami, including the thousands of children who were orphaned during this disaster. Working closely with the highly regarded Foundation for Children in Thailand (www.ffc.or.th), the Tsunami Children Foundation plans to implement a fully equipped, high-quality mental-health training program that will help the vast numbers of needy people there. (A program of this type does not currently exist in Thailand as "mental health issues" are traditionally looked down upon there.)

To learn more about the Tsunami Children Foundation, visit its website at www.tsunamicf.org

ABOUT THE AUTHOR

Born in Bangkok, the eldest of ten children, Tommy Tang left school at the age of eleven to help support his family. Driven early in life by the need to succeed, Tommy held a succession of odd jobs—floor-fan cleaner, welder, construction worker, busboy, boxer, auto mechanic, all the while helping his father with his restaurant in the Grand Central section of Bangkok—before he decided to emigrate to the United States in 1972.

While working as a rock band manager and completing his education at Palos Verde College in Southern California, Tommy found his true calling when he took a day job as manager and chef for a little-known Thai restaurant in Hollywood. For the most part, Thai cuisine was a total mystery to Americans at that time—within a year, thanks to Tommy's unique chef style, culinary talents, and brash entrepreneurial moxie, Thai dining became all the rage. It was the height of "the '70s," and Tommy's fantastic dishes were being heralded by world-class entertainment luminaries like Cher, Orson Welles, Jackson Browne, Robin Williams, and the rock group Queen among many others. It was during this time of first acclaim that Tommy met and married his wife, a marketing specialist who went on to become his partner in life and in business.

In 1982, just ten years after Tommy first came to America, he proved to be a trend-setting pied piper by establishing the original Tommy Tang's on Melrose Avenue in West Hollywood, California. Four years later, a second Tommy Tang's opened in New York City, making Tommy the first bi-coastal restaurant chef in the United States.

In the early 1990s, Tommy Tang made a splash in the world of book publishing—his first cookbook swiftly became a bestseller and played a major role in furthering the popularity of Thai cuisine in the United States. It was inevitable that Tommy would eventually wind up cooking on television, and in 1997, the PBS Network produced the first twenty-six of Tommy's cooking specials, which ran nationwide. To date, PBS has aired over 150 episodes globally. To learn more about Tommy's cooking program, visit www.tommytangs.com or www.letsgetcooking.org.

More than thirty years after first arriving in the United States as a smart and ambitious immigrant, Tommy Tang and his amazing success story remain a great testament to the rich flavor and variety of the American Dream.

INDEX

Clams (littleneck or Manila)
in Bangkok Jambalaya, 70
Malaysian, 93
in Seafood Pasta with Curry
Cream Sauce, 63
Coconut milk
in Alaska King Crab Curry,
76
basic recipe for, 112
in Blackened Scallops with
Roasted Garlic Chili
Sauce, 100
in Chicken Curry, 78
in Chicken Sate with Peanut
Sauce, 18
in Coconut Chili Sauce, 30
in Green Curry Salmon, 77
in Kaffir Lime Sauce, 88
in Lamb Mussamun, 79
in Lemon Grass Chicken, 84–
85
in Mussel Sate with Ginger
Cream Sauce, 20
overcooking of, 75
in Panang Chicken, 78–79
in Panang Curry Pasta with
Pine Nuts and Basil, 55
in Prik King Shrimp, 102
in Red Curry Shrimp, 75
in Roasted Chili Oysters, 96
in Rosemary Baby Lamb with
Curry Yogurt Sauce, 107
in Santa Fe Chili Pasta, 57
in Seafood Pasta with Curry
Cream Sauce, 63
in Shrimp Panang, 74
in Spicy BBQ Chicken with
Sweet Chili Sauce, 82
substitute for, 18
in Tiger Prawns with Cilantro
Cream Sauce, 104
in Tom Kha Kai, 34
Crabs
Alaska king
in California Roll, 15
curry, 76
snow
in Bangkok Jambalaya, 70
in Seafood Pasta with Curry
Cream Sauce, 63
in spring rolls, 24–25

soft-shell, with Garlic Ginger
Sauce, 92
Crab Spring Rolls with Santa Fe
Chili Yogurt Sauce, 24–
25
Crepes, Brunei Egg, 51
Cucumbers
in California Roll, 12
dip
basic recipe for, 8–9
for Thai Toast, 11
in Manhattan Roll, 12
in salad
Naked Shrimp Salad, 41
Thai Sausage Salad, 37
Curries
Alaska King Crab Curry,
76
chicken, 78
Panang, 78–79
Green Curry Salmon, 77
Lamb Mussamun, 79
Panang Curry Pasta with Pine
Nuts and Basil, 55
shrimp
Red Curry Shrimp, 75
Shrimp Panang, 74–75
Curry Cream Sauce, 63
Curry Fried Rice, 64
Curry Pasta, Panang, with Pine
Nuts and Basil, 55
Curry Yogurt Sauce, 107

Daikon sprouts, in Manhattan
Roll, 12
Dips, cucumber, 8–9
for Thai Toast, 11
Dried Chili Chicken, 85
Duck
Fried Rice, 67
The Original Tommy, with
Honey Ginger Sauce, 80–
81

Egg Crepes, Brunei, 51
Eggplant
in Green Curry Salmon, 77
with pine nuts, 46
Egg rolls, Thai, 22–23
Endive
in King Cobra, 30

in Spicy Beef Salad with
Lemon Grass Sauce, 42

Fish
in Bangkok Jambalaya, 70
in Thai Chili Fish, 87
See also Red Snapper; Salmon;
Tuna
Flying-fish roe, in Manhattan
Roll, 12
Fried rice, 64–69

Galanga
in Lemon Grass Stock, 110
in Tom Kha Kai, 34
Garlic Ginger Sauce, 92
Garlic Oyster Sauce, 49
Ginger Cream Sauce, 20, 98–99
Glaze, Rosemary Honey, 89
Green bell pepper puree, in
Green Curry Salmon, 77
Green Curry Salmon, 77
Grilled Fillet of Beef, 106
Grilled Red Snapper with
Rosemary Honey Glaze,
89
Grilled Salmon with Kaffir Lime
Sauce, 88
Grilled Tuna with Roasted Red
Bell Pepper Sauce, 90

Halibut, in Bangkok Jambalaya,
70
Honey Ginger Sauce, 80–81

Kaffir lime leaves
in Bangkok Jambalaya, 70
in Green Curry Salmon, 77
in Prik King Shrimp, 102
in Red Curry Shrimp, 75
in Roasted Chili Oysters, 96
Kaffir Lime Sauce, 88
King Cobra, 30
Kra-chai, in Green Curry Salmon,
77

Lamb, Rosemary Baby, with
Curry Yogurt Sauce, 107
Lamb Mussamun, 79
Larb, 29
Lard-na Noodles, 58

GOING WILD IN THE KITCHEN

The Fresh & Sassy Tastes of Vegetarian Cooking

Leslie Cerier

As vegetarianism's popularity continues to gain momentum, organic foods are making their way to the forefront of a health-conscious nation. Author and expert chef Leslie Cerier is crazy about the great taste and goodness of organically grown foods. In her latest cookbook, *Going Wild in the Kitchen,* Ms. Cerier shares scores of her favorite recipes that spotlight these fresh, wholesome foods.

Going Wild in the Kitchen is the first comprehensive global vegetarian cookbook to go beyond the standard organic beans, grains, and vegetables. In addition to providing helpful cooking tips and techniques, the book contains over 150 kitchen-tested recipes for healthful, taste-tempting dishes— creative masterpieces that contain such unique ingredients as edible flowers; sea vegetables; and wild mushrooms, berries, and herbs. It encourages the creative side of novice and seasoned cooks alike, prompting them to follow their instincts and "go wild" in the kitchen by adding, changing, or substituting ingredients in existing recipes. To help, a wealth of suggestions is found throughout. A list of organic foods sources completes this user-friendly cookbook.

Going Wild in the Kitchen is both a unique cookbook and a recipe for inspiration. So let yourself go! Excite your palate with this treasure-trove of unique, healthy, and taste-tempting recipe creations.

ABOUT THE AUTHOR

Leslie Cerier is a gourmet organic caterer, cooking instructor, and nutritional expert. She is the author of *The Quick and Easy Organic Gourmet* and coauthor of *Sea Vegetable Celebrations.* Ms. Cerier has published dozens of articles over the past fifteen years focusing on such topics as vegetarian cooking, nutrition, organic gardening, and natural living.

$16.95 US / $25.50 CAN • 240 pages • 7.5 x 9-inch quality paperback • 2-Color • ISBN 0-7570-0091-6

KITCHEN QUICKIES
Great, Satisfying Meals in Minutes
Marie Caratozzolo and Joanne Abrams

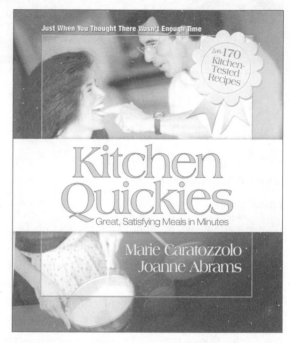

Have you ever left work after a long, hard day feeling totally exhausted, but knowing that the second you arrive home, you have to make a meal, *fast*? Or maybe you've spent the day driving your kids from soccer practice to play dates. Now everyone's clamoring for dinner. But is it possible to get a home-cooked meal on the table before, say, midnight? Absolutely!

The authors of *Kitchen Quickies* know that in this busy world, you just don't have time for hours of grocery shopping followed by hours of food preparation. Their solution? To begin with, virtually all of their over 170 kitchen-tested recipes call for a maximum of five ingredients other than kitchen staples. This makes shopping easier. Then the dish itself takes at most forty-five minutes to prepare. And these delicious dishes are actually good for you—low in fat and high in nutrients!

Kitchen Quickies begins by guiding you through the basics of quick-and-easy cooking. Following this are ten spectacular chapters filled with exciting and imaginative dishes, including sensational soups, satisfying sandwiches, refreshing salads, fabulous pastas, tempting chicken and turkey dishes, sizzling seafood, hearty beef and pork fare, meatless delights, enticing vegetable and grain side dishes, and luscious desserts. In *Kitchen Quickies,* you'll learn how to make tangy Margarita Chicken, Savory Crab Cakes, saucy Penne from Heaven, and more—all in no time flat!

So the next time you think that there's simply no time to cook a good meal, pick up *Kitchen Quickies.* Who knows? You may even have time for a few quickies of your own.

ABOUT THE AUTHORS
Marie Caratozzolo is a graduate of John Carroll University in Cleveland, Ohio, where she earned her BA in English, as well as a secondary teaching certificate. A wife and mother of two, Marie has been a book editor for over fifteen years.

Joanne Abrams earned her BA in English from the CW Post Campus of Long Island University. As an editor for over twenty years, and a cookbook editor for nearly a decade, Joanne has become proficient at preparing meals on the run.

$14.95 US / $20.95 CAN • 240 pages • 7.5 x 9-inch quality paperback • Full-Color Photos • ISBN 0-7570-0085-1

As You Like It Cookbook

Imaginative Gourmet Dishes with Exciting Vegetarian Options

Ron Pickarski

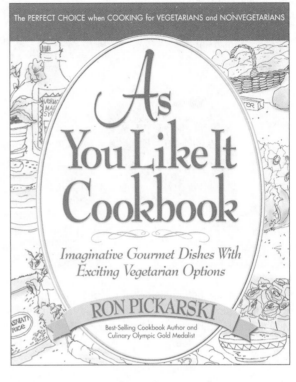

When it comes to food, we certainly like to have it our way. However, catering to individual tastes can pose quite a challenge for the cook. Have you ever prepared a wonderful dish, but because it contained beef or chicken, your daughter-in-law, the vegetarian, wouldn't go near it? To meet the challenge of cooking for vegetarians and nonvegetarians alike, celebrated chef Ron Pickarski has written the *As You Like It Cookbook.*

Designed to help you find the perfect meals for today's contemporary lifestyles, the *As You Like It Cookbook* offers over 175 great-tasting dishes that cater to a broad range of tastes. Many of the easy-to-follow recipes are already vegetarian—and offer ingredient alternatives for meat eaters. Conversely, recipes that include meat, poultry, or fish offer nonmeat ingredient options. Furthermore, if the recipe includes eggs or dairy products, a vegan alternative is given for those who follow a strictly plant-based diet. This book has it all—delicious breakfast favorites, satisfying soups and sandwiches, mouth-watering entrées and side dishes, and delectable desserts.

With one or two simple ingredient substitutions, the *As You Like It Cookbook* will show you how easy it is to transform satisfying meat dishes into delectable meatless fare, and vegetarian dishes into meat-lover's choices. It will guide you in making culinary decisions that result in meals that are gratifying and delicious, and cooked exactly as you (and your family) like them.

About the Author

Ron Pickarski is the first professional vegetarian chef to be certified executive chef by the American Culinary Federation, and is President and Chef/Consultant of Eco-Cuisine, Inc., a food technology consulting service. A recognized expert in the preparation of both traditional and vegetarian cuisine, Mr. Pickarski is also the author of *Eco-Cuisine: An Ecological Approach to Gourmet Vegetarian Cooking.*

$16.95 US / $25.50 CAN • 216 pages • 7.5 x 9-inch quality paperback • Full-Color Photos • ISBN 0-7570-0013-4

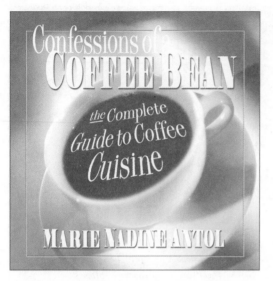

CONFESSIONS OF A COFFEE BEAN
The Complete Guide to Coffee Cuisine
Marie Nadine Antol

Yes, I have a few things to confess. But before I start, I just want you to know that I couldn't help it. It just happened. Everywhere I went, they wanted me. Whether it was my full body or my distinctive aroma, I can't tell you. All I know is that no matter where you go in this crazy mixed-up world, they all want coffee. Now, I have a few things to share—I think it's time to spill the beans.

Our love affair with coffee continues to blossom. From coast to coast, the growing number of coffee bars serves as a shining testament to this glorious romance. And now we have a wonderful new book that explores all things coffee. *Confessions of a Coffee Bean* is a complete guide to understanding and appreciating this object of our affection. It provides a fascinating history of the bean and its lore. It looks at the uniqueness of coffee houses found around the world—from Turkey to Germany to England. It details the various types of coffee available, as well as the best way to brew each to its own distinct perfection. It then concludes with over sixty enticing recipes that celebrate the very taste that is coffee.

$13.95 US / $20.95 CAN • 204 pages • 7.5 x 7.5-inch quality paperback • 2-Color • ISBN 0-7570-0020-7

FOR THE LOVE OF GARLIC
The Complete Guide to Garlic Cuisine
Victoria Renoux

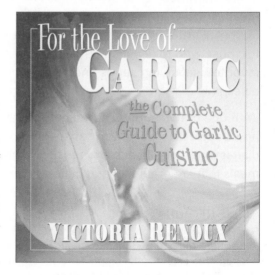

For the Love of Garlic is a celebration of an astonishingly versatile food. It explores garlic's past and present, and provides a wide variety of delicious kitchen-tested garlic recipes designed to tempt not only garlic aficionados, but all lovers of great cuisine.

Part One begins by looking at the history, lore, and many uses of this culinary treasure. It examines how garlic's active compounds have been proven to heal illness and maintain radiant health. Also included is a section on growing and buying this gourmet marvel. Part Two indulges in the tastes and pleasures of garlic. The author first discusses cooking techniques and special utensils that can enhance the use of this ingredient. She then offers eighty-five tempting dishes that will allow you to indulge all your garlic fantasies.

Whether given as a gift or used as a personal reference, this beautifully designed and illustrated work will prove itself to be a useful and informative guide time and time again.

$13.95 US / $20.95 CAN • 204 pages • 7.5 x 7.5-inch quality paperback • 2-Color • ISBN 0-7570-0087-8

TALES OF A TEA LEAF
The Complete Guide to Tea Cuisine
Jill Yates

For devoted tea drinkers everywhere, *Tales of a Tea Leaf*—a complete guide to the intricacies of tea lore, tea brewing, and tea cuisine—is here.

Part One of this book begins with an exploration of the legends and lore of tea. Read through the pages to discover intriguing details of tea's regal history, including its mysterious age-old relationship with rebels and smugglers. You will also learn of the many tea types and brewing methods, as well as the remarkable health benefits of the tea leaf. Part Two presents a collection of delicious tea beverages, from refreshing iced drinks to warm, spicy brews. And because tea is so much more than an amber-colored infusion, this book also offers many other wonderful tea creations, such as Apricot Tea Bread and Pumpkin Chai Pie.

You don't need to be a tea lover to enjoy *Tales of a Tea Leaf.* With nearly 3,000 varieties steeped in almost 5,000 years of history, tea and its fascinating story can be appreciated by everyone.

$13.95 US / $20.95 CAN • 204 pages • 7.5 x 7.5-inch quality paperback • 2-Color • ISBN 0-7570-0099-1

THE SOPHISTICATED OLIVE
The Complete Guide to Olive Cuisine
Marie Nadine Antol

Simple, elegant, refined. With a history as old as the Bible, the humble olive has matured into a sophisticated culinary treasure. Enter any fine restaurant and you will find the sumptuous flavor of olives in cocktails, appetizers, salads, and entrées. Now, food writer Marie Nadine Antol has created *The Sophisticated Olive*, an informative guide to this glorious fruit's many healthful benefits, surprising uses, and spectacular tastes.

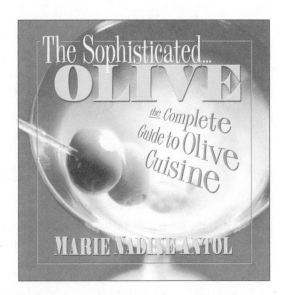

Part One begins by exploring the history of the olive and its range of remarkable properties, including its use as a beauty enhancer and health provider. It then goes on to describe the many olive varieties that are found throughout the world. Part Two presents over 100 kitchen-tested recipes, including salads, dressings, spreads, soups, side dishes, entrées, breads, and beverages—all designed to put a smile on the face of any olive lover.

$13.95 US / $20.95 CAN • 204 pages • 7.5 x 7.5-inch quality paperback • 2-Color • ISBN 0-7570-0024-X

THE MASON JAR COOKIE COOKBOOK

How to Create Mason Jar Cookie Mixes

Lonnette Parks

Nothing gladdens the heart like the tantalizing aroma of cookies baking in the oven. But for so many people, a busy lifestyle has made it impossible to find the time to bake at home—until now. Lonnette Parks, cookie baker extraordinaire, has not only developed fifty kitchen-tested recipes for delicious cookies, but has found a way for you to give the gift of home baking to everyone on your gift list.

For each mouth-watering cookie, the author provides the full recipe so that you can bake a variety of delights at home. In addition, she presents complete instructions for beautifully arranging the nonperishable ingredients in a Mason jar so that you can give the jar to a friend. By adding just a few common ingredients, your friend can then prepare fabulous home-baked cookies in a matter of minutes. Recipes include Best Ever Chocolate Chip Cookies, Blondies, and much, much more.

Whether you want to bake scrumptious cookies in your own kitchen or you'd like to give distinctive Mason jar cookie mixes to cookie-loving friends and family, *The Mason Jar Cookie Cookbook* is the perfect book.

$12.95 US / $21.00 CAN • 144 pages • 7.5 x 7.5-inch quality paperback • 2-Color • ISBN 0-7570-0046-0

THE MASON JAR SOUP-TO-NUTS COOKBOOK

How to Create Mason Jar Recipe Mixes

Lonnette Parks

In this follow-up to her best-selling book, *The Mason Jar Cookie Cookbook,* author and cook Lonnette Parks presents recipes for over fifty delicious soups, muffins, breads, cakes, pancakes, beverages, and more. And, just as in her previous book, the author tells you how to give the gift of home cooking to friends and family.

For each Mason jar creation, the author provides the full recipe so that you can cook and bake a variety of delights at home. In addition, she includes complete instructions for beautifully arranging the nonperishable ingredients in a Mason jar so that you can give the jar to a friend. Recipes include Golden Corn Bread, Double Chocolate Biscotti, Ginger Muffins, Apple Cinnamon Pancakes, Barley Rice Soup, Viennese Coffee, and much, much more.

$12.95 US / $21.00 CAN • 144 pages • 7.5 x 7.5-inch quality paperback • 2-Color • ISBN 0-7570-0129-7

**For more information about our books, visit our website at
www.squareonepublishers.com**